UNCOMMON DECENCY

Christian Civility
in an Uncivil World

RICHARD J. MOUW

INTERVARSITY PRESS
DOWNERS GROVE, ILLINOIS 60515

InterVarsity Press
P.O. Box 1400, Downers Grove, IL 60515-1426
World Wide Web: www.ivpress.com
E-mail: mail@ivpress.com

InterVarsity Press® *is the book-publishing division of InterVarsity Christian Fellowship/USA*®*, a student movement active on campus at hundreds of universities, colleges and schools of nursing in the United States of America, and a member movement of the International Fellowship of Evangelical Students. For information about local and regional activities, write Public Relations Dept., InterVarsity Christian Fellowship/USA, 6400 Schroeder Rd., P.O. Box 7895, Madison, WI 53707-7895, or visit the IVCF website at <www.intervarsity.org>.*

Scripture quotations, unless otherwise noted, are from the New Revised Standard Version of the Bible, copyright 1989 by the Division of Christian Education of the National Council of the Churches of Christ in the USA. Used by permission. All rights reserved.

ISBN 0-8308-1826-X

ISBN 0-8308-1825-1 (pbk.)

Printed in the United States of America ∞

Library of Congress Cataloging-in-Publication Data

Mouw, Richard J.
    Uncommon decency: Christian civility in an uncivil world / by
Richard Mouw.
        p. cm.
        ISBN 0-8308-1826-X.—ISBN 0-8308-1825-1 (pbk.)
        1. Church and the world. 2. Benevolence. 3. Courtesy—Biblical
teaching. I. Title.
    BR115.W6M68   1992
    241'.4—dc20

                                                                                        92-5680
                                                                                        CIP

P	24	23	22	21	20	19	18	17	16	15	14	13	12	11	10	9	8
Y	20	19	18	17	16	15	14	13	12	11	10	09	08	07	06	05	

Acknowledgments

This book could not have been written without the help and inspiration that I have received from many people. Two deserve special mention. Rodney Clapp at InterVarsity Press has been an uncommonly skilled editor. And my wife, Phyllis Gilbert Mouw, has been an uncommonly sensitive partner on an uncommonly decent journey.

1
Convicted Civility

Can We Be Faithful & Polite Too?

•   •   •

THE TWO CARS faced each other, bumpers almost touching and horns blaring. Neither driver was willing to yield.

It was a narrow city street, crowded tighter by several double-parked delivery trucks. The two drivers who had encountered each other in this obstacle course were both in an uncompromising mood. Finally one car edged forward, pushing the other backward. The driver of the nudged car angrily backed out of the way. But he quickly jumped out of the car and, as the other driver passed by, let loose a series of curses and obscene gestures.

Several of us who were passing along the street had stopped to watch this little drama. One woman offered a poignant assessment before she moved on: "Lordy, sometimes it makes you think that everything is falling apart!"

I don't know whether the woman on the sidewalk had ever read "The Second Coming," a poem written in 1921 by W. B. Yeats. But her image —"everything is falling apart"—is one that Yeats also used to express a sense of social crisis:

Things fall apart; the centre cannot hold;

Mere anarchy is loosed upon the world,

The blood-dimmed tide is loosed, and everywhere

The ceremony of innocence is drowned;

The best lack all conviction, while the worst

Are full of passionate intensity.[1]

Yeats and the woman on the sidewalk are not alone in their worries about trends in human relations. Laments about the loss of civility—simple politeness and courtesy—are common these days in editorials, articles, books and sermons.

I share that concern. Things really are falling apart. Common decency is on the wane. When challenged, people refuse to back off. They resent having to give others a little space. We talk past each other in many of our most important national and international discussions. Professions like law, medicine, education and finance have begun to lose the public trust. Violence is on the rise in our cities and villages. "Mere anarchy is loosed upon the world."

The angry encounter between the two drivers on the city street can be seen as a metaphor for the whole. There they all stand, bumper-to-bumper, horns blaring: pro-lifers and pro-choicers; gay liberationists and defenders of the traditional family; husbands and wives facing each other in courts of law; artists and legislators; "politically correct" intellectuals and crusading fundamentalists; warring ethnic groups in Eastern Europe; Irish Catholics and Irish Protestants; Arabs and Jews in the Middle East.

As a Christian I also worry that many believers seem to be contributing more to the problem than to the solution. Well-known clergy tell their followers that the time has come for a "battle" against the forces of unbelief. The TV cameras show Christians on the picket lines, angrily shaking their fists at their opponents. We are often good examples of the kind of difficult people whom Yeats described as being "full of passionate intensity."

When George Bush made a speech a few years ago calling Americans to be "a kinder, gentler people," I responded with a spirited "Amen!" And I thought kindness and gentleness should be especially characteristic of those of us who are Christians.

We were created for kind and gentle living. Indeed, kindness and gentleness are two of the "fruit-of-the-Spirit" characteristics that the apostle Paul mentions in Galatians 5. When Christians fail to measure up to the standards of kindness and gentleness, we are not the people God meant us to be.

Not Civility Alone

Not that civility is the be-all and end-all of life. We will not solve all our problems simply by becoming more civil people. There are times when it is appropriate to manifest some very uncivil feelings. "Passionate intensity" is not always out of place. If I am going to be a more civil person, it cannot be because I have learned to ignore my convictions.

A journalist hit the mark in a review essay dealing with urban problems. He said that Americans are facing a crisis in our cities because we "have let our standards of civility *and truth* waste dangerously away."[2] I am glad he included something about a lack of concern for the truth. It is not enough merely to reclaim civility. We need to cultivate a civility that does not play fast and loose with the truth.

As Martin Marty has observed, one of the real problems in modern life is that the people who are good at being civil often lack strong convictions and people who have strong convictions often lack civility.[3] I like that way of stating the issue. We need to find a way of combining a civil outlook with a "passionate intensity" about our convictions. The real challenge is to come up with a *convicted civility*.

"Inner" Civility

Civility is public politeness. It means that we display tact, moderation, refinement and good manners toward people who are different from us. It isn't enough, though, to make an outward show of politeness. Being civil has an "inner" side as well.

To be sure, for some people civility is only a form of play-acting. A friend was telling me about the difficult time he and his wife were experiencing in their relationship. "We go through whole weeks where we're lucky if we can simply manage to be *civil* to each other," he said. For him civility was not a very pleasant arrangement. It felt like a form of hypocrisy. Being civil meant that he and his wife would mask their hostile feelings with polite words and grudging accommodation.

In fact, my friend isn't alone. Many people today think of civility as nothing more than an outward, often hypocritical shell. But this cynical understanding of civility is yet another sign of the decline of real civility. In the past civility was understood in much richer terms. To be civil was to genuinely care about the larger society. It required a heartfelt commitment to your fellow-citizens. It was a willingness to promote the well-being of people who were very different, including people who seriously disagreed with you on important matters. Civility wasn't merely an external show of politeness. It included an inner politeness as well.

In *The Hiding Place* Corrie ten Boom tells of the time she and her father needed to find a safer place for a Jewish mother and child they had been concealing from the Nazis. A local clergyman came into their watch shop, and they asked him if he would take the Jews into his home. The pastor refused. On an impulse, Corrie ran to fetch the Jewish baby and brought it to him. But the pastor was not moved. "No. Definitely not," he said. "We could lose our lives for that Jewish child."

At that point, Father ten Boom stepped forward and took the baby into his own arms. He peered into the child's face for a moment, his white beard grazing against the tiny cheek. Then he looked up and spoke to the pastor: "You say we could lose our lives for this child. I would consider that the greatest honor that could come to my family."[4]

That was a wonderful display of civility. No mere outward show of politeness could have sustained the ten Booms through their fearful months of service to oppressed Jewish people. They had a deep and costly inner commitment to those God had identified as their neighbors, even though these neighbors represented a different cultural and religious ethos. Their civility was hardly an "empty shell."

Flourishing in Humanness

I already said that I believe being civil is a way of becoming more like what God intends us to be. Though he would not have put it in those terms, the ancient philosopher Aristotle would have agreed. He was firmly convinced that civility is necessary for people to realize their human potential. Along those lines, he insisted that we human beings are essentially "political animals." "Political" comes from the Greek word *polis,* which pertains to the city—like the Latin *civitas,* the root for our word "civil." Aristotle was convinced that we cannot become truly human until we can capably function as citizens of the city.

To be good citizens, we must learn to move beyond relationships that are based exclusively on familiarity and intimacy. We must learn how to behave among strangers, to treat people with courtesy not because we know them, but simply because we see them as human beings like ourselves. When we learn the skills of citizenship, Aristotle taught, we have begun to flourish in our humanness.

Acorns do not realize their innate possibilities until they grow branches and sprout leaves. And people do not attain their full potential until they learn how to behave in the public square. In their kind and brave treatment of their Jewish neighbors, Aristotle would have said, the ten Booms had learned some important lessons about what it means to be human.

The great Greek thinker's views on civility and citizenship have been echoed in the teachings of many Christians. St. Thomas Aquinas, for one, was convinced that the Bible confirmed Aristotle's philosophy on this subject. And John Calvin pursued a similar line of thought when he said that public life provides us with the opportunity "to shape our manners in accordance with civil justice."[5]

What Aristotle, Aquinas and Calvin are suggesting has profound implications for the way we make our way through the world. The woman on the sidewalk was expressing similar thoughts when she wondered aloud whether "everything is falling apart." She knew that the incivility she had witnessed on that cramped street was a deep violation of something important. If too much of that kind of thing happens, then we are on our way to losing our humanness. Things *will* fall apart.

The Struggle for Civility

But how can we hold onto strongly felt convictions while still nurturing a spirit that is authentically kind and gentle? Is it possible to keep these things together?

The answer is that it is not impossible—but it isn't easy. Convicted civility is something we have to work at. We have to work at it because both sides of the equation are very important. Civility is important. And so is conviction.

The Bible itself recognizes the difficulty of maintaining convicted civility. The writer of the epistle to the Hebrews lays the struggle out very clearly: we must "*pursue* peace with everyone," he tells us, while we work at the same time to cultivate that "holiness without which no one will see the Lord" (Heb 12:14).

For some of us, "pursuit" is a very appropriate image. Civility is an elusive goal. We have to chase after it, and the chasing seems never to end. We think we have finally caught it—and then civility slips from our grasp again. Just when we think we have figured out how we're going to live with the latest cult or how to tolerate the most recent public display of sexual "freedom," someone seems to up the ante; and the limits of our patience are tested all over again. So the pursuit goes on and on.

The Christian experience in North America has been one long pursuit of civility. When the earliest generations of North

American Christians were tempted by incivility, they were dealing primarily with their relationships with other Christians. Congregationalists had a hard time tolerating Baptists, and Roman Catholics fought with Presbyterians and Episcopalians. After a while, though, the skirmishes subsided; Protestants began to learn how to live in relative peace with each other, and with Catholics and Jews—as well as with the "fringe" types such as Mennonites and Quakers.

And then another set of problems emerged with newer religious movements. Mormons practiced polygamy. Shakers and other groups introduced novel patterns of communal living. Jehovah's Witnesses refused to allow their sick children to receive blood transfusions, and Christian Scientists rejected medical treatment altogether.

Traditional Christians gradually found ways of dealing with these challenges too. In some cases, as with Mormon polygamy, they set limits on what they would tolerate. With some groups they simply decided to live and let live. In other cases they worked out practical strategies for coping with specific excesses—adult Jehovah's Witnesses may refuse medical treatment for themselves, for instance, but when their children face life-threatening situations, they are temporarily made wards of the state so that the necessary transfusions can be given. After years of trial and error, a roughly acceptable arrangement was in place, and people with different religious beliefs and practices were able to live together with a fair degree of national harmony.

But the challenges of recent decades have sent us back to the drawing board. Now we have mosques in our neighborhoods and New Age devotees in our schools and businesses. Some professors openly call for a return to witchcraft and other ancient pagan practices. Homosexual couples want our churches to bless their "marriages." Cable television delivers pornography into our living rooms.

It is tempting to conclude that these developments have brought us to a point where civility is no longer possible. Isn't the social bond being stretched to the breaking point? Hasn't America's diversity reached proportions where we have lost any reasonable basis for living together in an atmosphere of tolerance and goodwill?

Perhaps. But as a Christian I am not ready to give up in despair. It has never been easy for the church to nurture a convicted civility. Indeed, when the biblical writer first urged the followers of Christ to "pursue peace with everyone," the society was at least as multicultural and pluralistic as ours is today. The early Christians were surrounded by a variety of religious and moral systems. Their pagan neighbors worshiped many gods, and that worship was sometimes so depraved that it would even be shocking in today's permissive culture. What would we think of a religious service in which men were ritually castrated? And the representatives of the dominant culture were not inclined to live-and-let-live when it came to dealing with the early Christian community.

Our forebears in the faith paid dearly for their commitment to the gospel. If they could work at treating people with gentleness and reverence in such an environment, what is our excuse for attempting less?

Promoting the Cause

There are two obvious ways to produce more people who combine strong convictions with a civil spirit: either we will have to help some civil people to become more convicted, or we will have to work at getting some convicted people to become more civil. Or *both,* since each of these strategies is important.

The first requires a kind of evangelism. We need to work at inviting the "nice" people in our society to ground their lives in robust convictions about the meaning of the gospel. But in order to do that, we have to be sure that we are doing our best to present discipleship as an attractive pattern of life. This means that we must also devote our energies to the second strategy: learning as Christians to be a gentler and more respectful people.

I admit that trying to make believers gentler and more "tolerant" will strike some Christians as wrong-headed. What about the devout, passionate people who picket abortion clinics and organize boycotts against offensive television programs? They might worry that becoming civil will mean a weakening of their faith. I am convinced that this is not necessarily so. Developing a convicted civility can help us become more mature Christians. Cultivating civility can make strong Christian convictions even stronger. That is what I want to try to show in these pages.

2
What
Christian
Civility
Is Not

• • •

I WAS TRYING out some of my ideas about convicted civility on a group of Christians in a retreat setting. As I presented my thoughts, I could tell that one woman was bothered by what I was saying. When it came time for group discussion, I asked her to speak up: "You look like something is troubling you. Would you like to tell me what it is?"

She paused before she responded: "My problem is that what you are saying makes good sense to me so far. But I'm worried about what you might be getting us into!"

Her worry was a legitimate one. I have my own fears when I hear people encouraging Christians to be more civil. Civility borders on many things, and some of them are problems. This is why I want to make it clear what I am *not* trying to "get us into" with all of this talk about civility.

Not Relativism

At a recent gathering of seminary professors, one teacher reported that at his school the most damaging charge one student can lodge against another is that the person is being "judgmental." He found this pattern very upsetting. "You can't get a good argument going in class anymore," he said. "As soon as somebody takes a stand on any important issue, someone else says that the person is being judgmental. And that's it. End of discussion. Everyone is intimidated!"

Many of the other professors nodded knowingly. There seemed to be a consensus that the fear of being judgmental has taken on epidemic proportions.

Is the call for civility just another way of spreading this epidemic? If so, then I'm against civility. But I really don't think that this is what being civil is all about.

Christian civility does not commit us to a *relativistic* perspective. Being civil doesn't mean that we cannot criticize what goes on around us. Civility doesn't require us to *approve* of what other people believe and do. It is one thing to insist that other people *have the right* to express their basic convictions; it is another thing to say that they *are right* in doing so. Civility requires us to live by the first of these principles. But it does not commit us to the second formula. To say that all beliefs and values deserve to be treated as if they were on a par is to endorse relativism—a perspective that is incompatible with Christian faith and practice.

Christian civility does not mean refusing to make judgments

about what is good and true. For one thing, it really isn't possible to be completely nonjudgmental. Even telling someone else that she is being judgmental is a rather judgmental thing to do!

And suppose we *could* actually suspend judgment about other people's beliefs and values. Would that be a desirable thing to do? The Bible regularly tells us to exercise judgment about questions of truth and value: "Woe to those who call evil good and good evil" (Is 5:20 NIV); "test the spirits to see whether they are from God" (1 Jn 4:1). Indeed, in the very same passage in which the apostle Paul calls us to cultivate kindness, patience and generosity, he insists that we take a strong stand against such "works of the flesh" as sexual immorality, impurity and drunkenness (Gal 5:16-23). So it seems Christians can hardly avoid "judging" certain attitudes and behaviors.

At the same time, there are many texts that apparently lean against judgment. Didn't Jesus himself tell us, "Do not judge, so that you may not be judged"? And didn't our Lord show us what this means by his own example, accepting people just the way they were—including prostitutes and tax collectors, who were generally considered to be very undesirable types?

Those are important questions. But they do not get at a real conflict between the example of Jesus and the "judgmental" texts in the Bible. In both cases where Jesus is recorded as commanding us not to judge, he was warning against a certain kind of judgmental spirit. In Matthew's account he is speaking about hypocritical people who criticize others without paying attention to their own faults, and in Luke's Gospel Jesus is referring to people who criticize others with a condemning and unforgiving spirit (Mt 7:1-5; Lk 6:37-38).

Similarly, we must pay close attention to the *sense* in which

Jesus accepted people just as they were. Much of the loose talk these days about "accepting" and "affirming" people is very different from Jesus' patterns. Certainly there is nothing in his example or teachings that would tell us not to try to change people's lives. In one way, perhaps Jesus wants us to "affirm" heroin dealers and to "accept" members of the Ku Klux Klan just as they are—but surely that doesn't mean we should make our peace with drug-trafficking and racist crusades!

When Jesus showed "acceptance" to prostitutes and tax collectors, he did not condone their sexual or economic behaviors. He loved them *in spite of* their unsavory ways. He called Mary Magdalene and Zacchaeus to correct their ways and become faithful disciples.

But Jesus refused to define people in terms of their present sordid circumstances. He affirmed their *potential* for living as faithful and creative children of God.

That is the kind of free and open acceptance we owe to people. A relativistic embrace of anything others do is no favor to them. It is not genuine Christian civility.

Not Liking Everyone

When I told a friend that I was writing a book on civility, he winced. "Oh, no," he said. "I never thought that you would join the 'feel good' crowd. Whatever happened to the good old days when we could just dislike some people without having to feel guilty about it?"

I'm not preaching a message about having positive feelings about everyone. To be civil toward people does not mean that we have to *like* them.

As I write this, my thoughts quickly move to a person whom I find very unlikable. Instinct tells me that try as I might, I will never be able to like him. But my instinct could easily be a sinful one. Maybe I could learn to like him, although it would certainly require much time and effort. Civility is a different matter, though. I can treat this person with gentleness and respect even if I haven't manufactured those feelings that would count as "liking" him.

I learned a good lesson on this subject from a crusty old Irish Catholic judge who spoke at a conference on the ministry of the laity. His assignment was to tell how his life in the legal system is influenced by his Christian faith.

As he began his speech, he sounded almost cynical. His days are filled with the routine and not-so-routine patterns of inner-city crime, and he confessed that he found it very difficult to see many connections between the gospel and his courtroom decisions.

Then he went on to tell us of a recent experience. In a Sunday-morning homily, his parish priest had talked about the importance of seeing things through the eyes of Jesus. Sometime during the next week, the priest encouraged the congregation, stop and ask yourself how Jesus would view the situation you are presently in.

A few days later a young man from the inner city appeared before the judge's bench. He had been there several times before. "I was ready to give him a rather harsh sentence," the judge said. "Then suddenly I remembered the priest's words. I stopped and asked myself, What would Jesus see if he were sitting in my place?

"I decided that he would see a young person with much street-savvy, who is using his considerable intelligence and skill to get the most he can from a social system that he feels is stacked against him. I looked this young man in the eye and told

him that I thought he was a bright and talented human being.
And then I said to him, 'Let's talk together about how we can
get you living in more creative and constructive ways.'

"We had a surprisingly good conversation. I don't know
whether it will do much good in the long run, but for once I
think I really did act in a Christlike manner in the courtroom!"

This judge had done more than deal with the young man in
terms of a formal kind of "honoring." He had actually shown
him a gentleness and a reverence. Does this mean that he had
quickly learned to like the young man? Probably not—but liking him was not really necessary.

What the judge had done was to reflect upon this young
man's *value and potential.* And this same attitude is what I owe
to the person whom I find it impossible to like. I can choose to
concentrate, not on his disagreeable characteristics, but on the
value and potential he has in the sight of God.

Every human being is a center of value. The value may not
always be obvious to us. This is why we have to go out of our
way to reflect upon the value of specific human beings. We
Christians can do this by reminding ourselves that the person
in question is created by God. If an artist friend produces a
work of art that I don't particularly like, I can still treat that
artifact with reverence if I remind myself of the value it has
for the person who made it. The more I respect the artist, the
more I will go out of my way to revere her work.

Every human being is a work of divine art. God has crafted
each of us; we are all "special creations." Even when we have
rebelled against God and distorted his handiwork in our lives,
he continues to love us—much as an artist loves something
which she has worked on lovingly, even when it has been severely damaged. I can learn a lot about how to treat an unlikable

person with reverence if I keep reminding myself of the value the person has in the eyes of God.

And I can also concentrate on people's potential rather than their present disagreeable condition. The judge did not necessarily like the young man standing before him; but he did admire what the young man *could* be. Reflecting upon people's capabilities for betterment is a way of cultivating a gentle and reverent spirit toward them.

Not Nationalism

But let's go back to the two angry drivers on the narrow city street. They don't have time to reflect on each other's God-given potential. For them to become more civil is to learn to be kind and gentle in brief encounters with total strangers.

We must not lose sight of this very public dimension of civility. Being civil isn't just trying to be respectful toward the people we know. It is also to care about our *common life*. It involves not only working hard at close relationships but also cultivating a deep concern for the *civitas,* for the way things go in our public spaces—on sidewalks and highways, at football games and national parks, in malls and legislatures.

Here too there are some excesses that we should worry about. Caring about our common life can take on a dangerous shape. Some Christians seem to think the only way to show a genuine love for the public square is to cultivate a passionate and uncritical devotion to their nation.

This is not what I mean by civility. Being civil does not require us to be superpatriots. From a Christian point of view, that would not be a very healthy thing to advocate.

To honor your nation—your "fatherland" or "motherland"— is a legitimate thing. There can be something very noble and healthy about patriotic sentiments, just as there is something good about nurturing positive sentiments for our parents. We don't even need to worry if these sentiments get expressed with a little exaggeration. I don't get upset when I hear someone say to her parents on a special occasion, "You are the most wonderful mom and dad in the whole world!" Our patriotic expressions can be viewed in the same way: sometimes it's a good thing to get carried away with enthusiasm for the nation that "births" us as citizens.

The problem comes, of course, when our nationalistic statements are not meant as affectionate hyperbole. I would be very nervous about a person who is absolutely sure that her parents simply *are* the best mom and dad in the whole world. I have even bigger worries about people who feel that way about their own nation.

The Best Parents case does not pose a serious threat to others. The daughter may *believe* that her parents are actually superior to all other parents, and she may look with disdain on everyone who has a special affection for another set of parents. But her attitude is not likely to grow into anything more than an isolated case of weirdness.

The threat is much bigger, though, when people start singing the Best Nation song with intense seriousness. Nations often want things that belong to other nations. Nations have armies, and armies use weapons. When a specific nation starts thinking of itself as Number One In The World, it is time to start worrying.

But from a Christian point of view the problem starts with the attitude itself, quite apart from any bad consequences that may flow from it. My nation does not deserve my uncritical loyalty. No country should ever be encouraged actually to think of itself in Best Nation terms.

Nationalism and superpatriotism are forms of idolatry. And the Bible makes it very clear that this is the kind of idolatrous attachment that Jesus wants to free us from. Christians are being gathered into a new kind of community in which all the older allegiances of our present world begin to take second place:

> After this I looked, and there was a great multitude that no one could count, from every nation, from all tribes and peoples and languages, standing before the throne and before the Lamb, robed in white, with palm branches in their hands. They cried out in a loud voice, saying,
>
> "Salvation belongs to our God who is seated on the throne, and to the Lamb!" (Rev 7:9-10)

Not an Evangelistic Strategy

As a college student, I was returning to school one year on a Greyhound bus. One of the other passengers was a middle-aged man who seemed to be making the rounds, engaging various people in quiet conversation. Walking down the aisle, he would exchange pleasantries with a person, and if the person seemed willing he would sit down and talk a while.

Finally it was my turn. We chatted for about fifteen minutes; he asked me questions about myself—family, studies, hobbies. Then the conversation took an abrupt and rather forced turn toward religion; as I remember it, he went quickly from remarking on the heat of the noonday sun to a comment about the warm love of the Son of God.

I immediately told him I was a Christian. His irritated retort caught me off-guard: "I wish you would have told me that a little earlier!" Then he got up and walked down the aisle, looking for another conversation partner.

I hope there are not too many Greyhound evangelists who operate with that style. But the encounter, crude as it was, illustrates a point. This Christian man's "civility" was a mere ploy. His questions about my family, studies and hobbies were quite insincere. Someone had probably told him that evangelism works best when you show an interest in the other person. So he "showed an interest" in me for fifteen minutes before he made his move. I felt manipulated. And I would not blame a non-Christian if she too felt very manipulated by this person's approach.

Christians need to be careful about seeing civility as a mere strategy for evangelism. As an evangelical Christian I want to be careful not to be misunderstood as I make this point. I want people to accept the evangel, the good news of salvation through Jesus Christ. I place a high priority on the evangelistic task. But this does not mean that Christian civility is simply an evangelistic ploy—being nice to people merely because we want them to become Christians.

Evangelism is an important activity. The apostle Peter tells us that we should always be ready to give an account to anyone of the hope that lives in our hearts. But he immediately adds: "Yet do it with gentleness and reverence" (1 Pet 3:15-16). I did not feel that I was treated gently and reverently by the evangelist on the bus.

Civility has its own value, quite apart from any evangelistic or political results it might produce. To become a gentler and more reverent person is itself a way of being more like what God intended us to be.

Does that seem like a provocative thought—maybe even a questionable one? I suspect that it will for many sincere Christians. Reverence toward others is not an attitude that has been highly prized in the Christian community. We need to look at how to state the case for civility in a way that will be convincing for people who take the gospel seriously.

3
Defending Christian Civility

• • •

MANY CHRISTIANS OF the past were crusaders who had no use for civility. Indeed, most Christian groups have at least a few crusaders in their galleries of heroes and heroines.

I read an account recently about such a person in my own Calvinist tradition. It was not too long after the Reformation, and he wanted everyone in his country to worship in the manner he thought was right. He was so dead set against compromise on this subject that he took up arms to defend his cause. He was captured and was given a choice: agree to compromise or face a martyr's death. He chose martyrdom.

His dying speech was predictably unyielding. If we are willing to tolerate different religious viewpoints, he said, that can only mean one of two things—either we care very little about the truth or we do not worry much about other people's eternal souls. Either of these attitudes, he insisted, is abominable.

I have mixed feelings about this kind of speech. On the one hand, I am convinced that this man was misguided when he refused to practice tolerance; I do not believe that it's abominable for me to tolerate people with different convictions from mine. But I admire some of what he affirms. Many of my own theological convictions are similar to his. And like him, I think it's a good thing to have firm convictions about such matters.

To struggle with a case like this is no mere exercise in ivory-tower speculation for me. This man has spiritual descendants today. They may not think a certain form of worship should be mandated by force, but they worry that any concession to civility is a very dangerous business.

You don't have to spend too many minutes tuned in to Christian programs on radio or television to hear anticivility sentiments:

☐ "We are in a battle for the soul of our nation!"

☐ "There can be no compromise with falsehood!"

☐ "Satan's favorite words are 'toleration' and 'pluralism'!"

But it isn't just people on the "right" who are anticivil. Opponents of civility can also be found on the Christian "left":

☐ "The enemies of liberation must be confronted without fear!"

☐ "The struggle for justice is too urgent for us to worry about being nice!"

Is there anything convincing I can say to such persons? Suppose they were willing to spend a little time listening carefully to the best biblical case we can produce in favor of civility—what could I ask them to consider?

Public Christianity

Let's begin to answer this question by looking at what we can affirm in the crusaders' perspective. This will help us to be clear about some basics.

God cares about public righteousness. Give the anticivility folks the benefit of the doubt. They want very much to please God. And they are convinced that God is deeply interested in what goes on in the public realm. Here is where Jerry Falwell and Tim LaHaye and the liberation theologians are all on the right track. To be sure, they are wrong in thinking that God is especially fond of societies in which everyone holds strictly to their point of view. But they are not wrong to think that the God of the Bible is committed to public righteousness.

Some Christians have tried to reduce the gospel to a purely individual message. That is unfortunate, and many of the anticivility people are very clear about this fact. The gospel *is* good news for individuals, but it is also more than that. It is good news for societies—indeed, for the whole creation. Isaac Watts put it well in his ever-popular Christmas carol: the power of the gospel is meant to reach "far as the curse is found."

God doesn't like cursedness. It grieves him when governments are corrupt, and when people cheat and blaspheme and lie. He sent Jesus into the world to deliver us from all of this. Some of us have already experienced clear signs of that deliverance in our own personal pilgrimages. But we know that the problems have not yet gone away, on either the individual or the corporate level. And so we long for a more comprehensive deliverance. We want God to make everything right. And God has promised to do that.

Christians are called to be agents of God's righteousness. The Calvinist martyr and his fellow-travelers are not only aware of God's promise to make everything right. They also rightly sense an obligation to participate in that program of righteousness.

Different Christian groups emphasize different things when they explain God's concern for public righteousness. Pat Robertson wants an orderly society in which children are raised in healthy families and the public schools promote a morality based on the Ten Commandments. The "radical" Christians emphasize the call to peacemaking and justice.

Actually, all of these concerns are important. And they are interconnected. A righteous society is one that fosters character development and where peace and justice hold sway.

The biblical writers often make this point by telling us that God wants a world filled with *shalom*. This word is usually translated "peace," but it points to something much richer than a mere absence of conflict. When *shalom* happens, everything is functioning in the way the Creator intended. People are flourishing as they take delight in doing God's will. So Christian disciples should have a part in promoting this divine *shalom*.

As agents of righteousness, we must try to bring God's standards to bear on public life. The anticivility folks may be a little too sure of their own ability to figure out exactly what God wants to do with the societies in which they live—but they are not wrong in their conviction that God's will is applicable to the issues of public life.

There is room for genuine disagreement among Christians about the details of public righteousness. Pacifists and just-war defenders can both be deeply committed to peacemaking. Advocates of a strong free-market system can be as concerned about the poor and the helpless as liberation theologians are. The biblical message is rich and complex, and it was first addressed to Ancient Near Eastern cultures. It takes some work to discern how to apply it properly to contemporary life. Passionate arguments among Christians, when they are pursued in a nonideological manner, can be a helpful way of working through the difficult questions.

And we do not need to despair of finding solutions—especially if we are willing to settle for provisional and partial ones. The general standards of divine righteousness are very clear: there can be no doubt, for example, that God is concerned about truth and faithfulness and love. We will not be left with endless confusion as we seek to apply these standards to the dilemmas of contemporary discipleship. By carefully studying the Scriptures, and by consulting our consciences and engaging in dialog with others, we can often be fairly confident about the merits of specific strategies and programs.

Imitating the Divine Character

I think that many of the anticivility people would agree with these basics. But they would find nothing here to cure them of their incivility. How do we introduce a gentler Christianity into this picture? To answer this question, we must add some items to our list of basics.

God has a gentle and reverent concern for public righteousness. The question of the divine character is crucial to our topic. Christian anticivility is grounded in a failure to understand God's own civility. Many convicted Christians place a central emphasis on the harsher side of the Bible's portrayal of God's character: sovereignty, holiness, power, wrath and the like.

I, too, believe that God possesses these traits. I have no interest in trying to "tame" the God of the Bible. God is a sovereign ruler—but in Jesus Christ he made it clear that he is that rare kind of ruler who comes to his people in the form of a servant. God is holy—but his holiness is revealed in his love for us. God is all-powerful—but his supreme power is displayed in the weakness and vulnerability of the cross. God is a God of wrath—but he is also "slow to anger and abounding in steadfast love and faithfulness" (Ps 86:15).

As agents of God's righteousness, we are called to imitate the divine character. In our efforts at public discipleship, we need to cultivate the traits that are associated with God's own kindness and gentleness.

During a friendly argument I was having with a Catholic theologian about the Virgin Mary, he told me a little legend that he had heard as a child. A man died with some unconfessed sin on his conscience. When he arrived at the gates of heaven, God angrily chided him and told him to go spend time in purgatory. The Holy Mother overheard the conversation, and when God was not looking she sneaked the man into heaven through a back door.

My theologian friend's point was significant. Because Catholic theology has often pictured God as a harsh and unyielding Judge, Mary has served to "soften" our understanding of the divine holiness.

Roman Catholics are not the only ones whose functional understanding of God has needed some softening. Of course, the solution to this distorted theology (and my Catholic friend agreed with me on this) is to correct our view of God. God is not a distant and unapproachable despot. The kindness and gentleness of the Mary portrayed in traditional spirituality is not a necessary *corrective* to the divine nature—it is a *reflection* of that nature. This is one of the important lessons we learn from the redemptive ministry of that kind and gentle One who said to his disciples, "Whoever has seen me has seen the Father" (Jn 14:9).

And we in turn are called to be Christlike. This means that we too are called to reflect the kindness and gentleness of God.

Our efforts at public righteousness must be modest ones. Now this is a dangerous point to emphasize. The call to modesty can easily be interpreted as giving Christians permission to be unconcerned about the issues of public life. "Poverty is always with us, so why worry about injustices?" "You're never really going to do away with prejudice and conflict—at least not until Jesus returns!" We may hear statements like these when we start encouraging modesty. But the risk is necessary, especially in the light of the immodesty that has often characterized Christian forays into the public arena.

The Calvinist martyr's speech was immodest. Toleration, he said, is an abominable attitude. No compromise is acceptable. Those who adopt our variety of Christianity are possessors of the truth, and everyone else is caught up in error.

We can avoid this harshness if we work at remembering where we are in God's scheme of things. Christians, like everyone else, are finite creatures living in a time when God has not yet filled the world with his *shalom.* We are in a period of waiting. Not a passive waiting—we must act even as we wait for the final resolution of the cosmic drama. But we act in the knowledge that the most we can hope for in this present time is signs or "first fruits" of the ultimate victory.

In an important sense, this means Christians should endorse toleration and compromise. Not that we can elevate these qualities to the level of absolute principles. No Christian can promise to tolerate anything that comes along. Nor can we commit ourselves to compromise as a way of life.

But as people who are in the process of cultivating convicted civility, we will operate with a strong bias in favor of toleration.

Our ability to tolerate other convictions and lifestyles will have moral limits, but we will be careful not to decide too quickly that we have reached those limits. And within the limits, we can compromise.

I was cured of my prejudice against the word *compromise* a few decades ago. I listened to a lecture by a "radical Christian" who spent several minutes criticizing Christians who were willing to compromise with the "exploitative capitalist system." True discipleship, he insisted, does not engage in any sort of compromise.

But a little later, he turned to a critique of the "legalism" of traditional Christianity. He began to preach about the need for "flexibility" in response to the "ambiguities" and "complexities" of our sinful existence. I decided that he would have been more honest if he had admitted that he favored some kinds of compromise and opposed others.

I have a formula to offer for attaining Christian modesty: *each of us must attempt to be faithful in the situations where God has placed us and with the resources God has made available to us.* The world has already been visited by one overwhelmingly adequate Messiah. No more would-be messiahs need apply. Our calling is not to bring the kingdom of God in its fullness; it is to witness to the power and presence of that kingdom in ways that are made available to us.

The church is our primary context for learning public righteousness. The sermons that we Christians preach to the larger world about righteousness will not mean much if we do not ourselves display something of that righteousness. Christians are a people who are in the process of being "made right" by the grace of God. And this righteousness is not meant to be only something that we possess as individuals. To be a Christian is to belong to a community that is the process of being "made right."

This means our message to the larger society will be credible only if we can invite others to become more like us. I know that sounds arrogant. But if we are not able to point to our own communal life to illustrate the righteousness we want for everyone, our message is not credible.

Jesus' words on this subject echo through the New Testament: "You are the light of the world. A city built on a hill cannot be hid. . . . Let your light shine before others, so that they may see your good works and give glory to your Father in heaven" (Mt 5:14-16).

The Scope of Civility

No Christian denies that there are "niceness" themes in the Bible. The passages that encourage us to develop kindness and gentleness are difficult to ignore completely. But that still leaves us with questions about the *scope* of Christian civility.

"Scope" questions loom large in Christians' discussions about how we are to behave. For example, I have heard people argue that while the Bible does indeed call us to come to the aid of the poor, it is really only the *Christian* poor whom we should care about. The same kind of question applies to kindness themes. "Error has no rights" is an old slogan in Christian social thought.

It is legitimate to ask who is entitled to our gentleness and reverence. "They'll know we are Christians by our love"—but love toward *whom*? How far do we go with Christian civility?

We will pursue this "scope" question in detail in later chapters. But we can lay out some key biblical considerations here.

In the Old Testament, Israel was called to be a very special kind of national community. This same call is applied in the New Testament to the Christian church: the followers of Jesus are to act like "a holy nation" (1 Pet 2:9). All Christians have a dual citizenship; in St. Augustine's famous formulation, we belong to both the City of Man and the City of God. We may have legal citizenship in the United States or Nigeria or Peru or Thailand or Sweden; but we are also bound together into a transnational, multiethnic community of people whose supreme allegiance is to the lordship of Jesus Christ. This allegiance gives us our primary "national" identity. In the deepest sense, it defines who we are.

When we think about how we treat other Christians, then, we are addressing issues of "domestic policy." The question of how we relate to people who are not believers is a matter of our "foreign policy." The Bible gives us some clear guidance on foreign policy issues.

The treatment of strangers. Sometimes the patterns of Old Testament life are depicted as very uncivil. But much more needs to be said. For example, the people of Israel were regularly instructed to go out of their way to show respect to strangers. The "stranger" (or "sojourner" or "alien") referred to in the Old Testament was typically a person from a different ethnic and religious group. The Israelites regularly encountered such people, either as travelers passing through the land or as resident aliens in Israel.

These strangers, God said, were to receive kind and considerate treatment. Leviticus 19 makes the point very clearly: do no wrong to strangers; treat them as if they were natives; love them as you love yourselves. And lest the point be missed, God reminded the Israelites of the time when they were on the receiving end: "for you were aliens in the land of Egypt:

I am the LORD your God" (v. 34).

This is the biblical analog to Aristotle's insistence that we become more fully human when we learn to function as citizens in the public square. When we respect the stranger, we go beyond the bonds of intimacy and kinship.

Here is an important lesson for our present-day world, which is so torn apart by ethnic, racial and religious antagonisms. God wants us to offer a fundamental respect to others purely on the basis of their humanness. Christians and Muslims, African Americans and Jewish Americans, heterosexuals and homosexuals, rich and poor—all are created in the divine likeness. In affirming the stranger, we are honoring the image of God.

The welfare of the city. When the children of Israel were taken off to Babylon as captives, they faced some serious questions about civility. For a long time they had been living in their own land, with familiar rulers and institutions. They had experienced the unity of a people who were committed (officially at least!) to obeying the will of God in all aspects of their lives.

But now they were aliens in a strange environment, surrounded by a pervasively pagan culture. Psalm 137 records their poignant plea: "How could we sing the LORD's song in a foreign land?" (v. 4). God answered their query through the prophet Jeremiah. You are to settle into the land for the long haul, the prophet told the people: construct homes to live in, raise crops, get married and have children; "multiply there, and do not decrease" (Jer 29:4-6). And then a very important "policy statement" is added: "But seek the welfare of the city where I have sent you into exile, and pray to the LORD on its behalf, for in its welfare you will find your welfare" (v. 7).

This is a call to civility. God is telling the Israelites—and us—that neither indifference nor hostility is a proper way of treating our pagan neighbors. We must seek their welfare. Indeed, it is in pursuing the well-being of others that we realize our own well-being.

Christlike compassion. Jesus' incarnational ministry may not always seem to be relevant to our life as citizens. As a result, important resources for the public behavior of the Christian community are neglected. The Old Testament patterns of kindness to the stranger and concern for the welfare of society had concrete embodiment in the ministry of Jesus.

This point was reinforced for me one afternoon when my subconscious was apparently working overtime. I was driving to the airport, on my way to give a speech somewhere on the subject of Christianity and politics. As I reviewed the outline of my speech, I began to hum quietly. Suddenly I realized that I was humming the refrain of a song I had not sung since my youth. I began to sing the words:

Be like Jesus, this my song,
In the home and in the throng.
Be like Jesus all day long
I would be like Jesus.

I had never thought of the Christian's public calling in quite that way before—to act in a Christlike manner "in the throng." And as I began to review how Jesus acted in public places, I realized that kindness and gentleness pervaded these encounters.

It is an interesting exercise to go through the Gospel accounts, paying specific attention to all the references to "the crowds." You will find Jesus regularly surprising people as he pays special attention to the seemingly insignificant individuals who cry out to him in the midst of crowded places.

But Jesus also shows a loving interest in the crowds as such. My favorite example is a wonderful passage at the end of

Matthew 9. Jesus has paid quite a bit of attention to individuals in this chapter: he has healed a paralytic, enlisted a despised tax collector as his disciple, cured two blind men and liberated a demon-possessed man. Then, after all of that, he encounters the teeming human masses: "When he saw the crowds, he had compassion for them, because they were harassed and helpless, like sheep without a shepherd" (Mt 9:36).

This brief sentence is heavy with meaning. The people of Israel had from ancient times awaited a ruler who "will feed his flock like a shepherd; . . . [and] will gather the lambs in his arms, and carry them in his bosom, and gently lead the mother sheep" (Is 40:11). Jesus is the fulfillment of that deep yearning. In his shepherdlike compassion for the crowds, he is showing himself to be more than a savior of individuals. He is also the healer of our public spaces.

This does not mean that we Christians should cast ourselves in the role of political shepherds who are sent into the world to save all the confused "sheep" of our society. That would be arrogant—we too are sheep who need the Shepherd's gentle care. But we *can* reflect on the ways in which we model a Christlike compassion in contemporary society, as suggested in another hymn that deals with being like Jesus "in the throng":

Where cross the crowded ways of life,
Where sound the cries of race and clan,
Above the noise of selfish strife,
We hear your voice, O Son of Man.

In haunts of wretchedness and need,
On shadowed thresholds dark with fears,
From paths where hide the lures of greed,
We catch the vision of your tears.

Christians and "everyone." The New Testament Epistles were written to Christians who were living in various parts of the Roman Empire. These believers' questions were similar to those of the Old Testament Jews who were exiled in Babylon: How do we handle the fact that we are surrounded by pagans? How do we act toward people with whom we have little in common—and who are sometimes even overtly hostile to us?

The apostolic teachers took these questions seriously. Over and over again they gave instructions on how Christians were to treat "everyone" and "all people." Here is the apostle Paul on the subject: "If it is possible, so far as it depends on you, live peaceably with all" (Rom 12:18). And Paul's coworker Titus advised Christians "to speak evil of no one, to avoid quarreling, to be gentle, and to show every courtesy to everyone" (Tit 3:2).

How to relate to unbelievers is an important topic in St. Peter's letters. At one point he puts the case in very direct, simple terms: "Honor everyone" (1 Pet 2:17). "Honoring" here means having an active regard for someone's well-being. Not that we are simply to give people what they ask for or tell them only what they want to hear. The apostle is not prescribing convictionless civility. But even when we speak directly about our convictions, he warns, we must do so in the proper spirit: "Always be ready to make your defense to anyone who demands from you an accounting for the hope that is in you; yet do it with gentleness and reverence" (1 Pet 3:15-16). This is what civility is all about: honoring other people—even people whose beliefs and actions we dislike—in a manner that is gentle and reverent.

Once again, the example of Jesus is very much to the point. But not just his treatment of other people. We must also think about the way he treats *us*. An old gospel song tells us that when Jesus calls us to repent, he does so "softly and tenderly." That experience gives us our most important model of civility. Jesus loves us even when we are unlovable. The Good Shepherd has patiently searched for his wayward sheep. We have been honored by a divine gentleness and reverence that is beyond comprehension. Having experienced this tenderness, how can we not care deeply about civility?

4
Speaking in God's Presence

The Importance of Civil Speech

• • •

ALL THAT I EVER really needed to know about uncivil language I learned in the fifth grade.

At a small Dutch Calvinist school in a New Jersey city, I was playing with other students just before classes started. Some black kids came by on their way to the public school. One thing led to another, and soon our two groups were yelling insults at each other. One of the black students tossed a rock, and it grazed my head. I was livid. I spat out the "N" word and ran back to school.

This was the early 1950s, and we weren't thinking much about civil rights in those days. But the young stone-thrower must have sensed that he had a case to make: he marched straight to my school and reported my verbal behavior to the principal.

Soon the principal and I were facing each other, alone in his office. Mr. Dykstra told me how disappointed he was with me. I began to cry: "But he threw a *stone* at me! He *hit* me with it!"

Mr. Dykstra's response was kind but firm. "Yes, he shouldn't have done that. I'm sorry it happened to you. But Richard, you have done something much worse. He tried to harm your body. You responded by trying to harm his soul. God is much more saddened by what you did to that young man than by what he did to you."

Mr. Dykstra's preferred means of punishment was to assign "lines"—writing a prescribed resolution such as "Never again will I chew bubble gum in class" fifty or a hundred times over. In the more serious cases the miscreant had to have the final product signed by a parent.

My punishment for saying the "N" word established a new record for "lines" writing at the Riverside Christian School. I had to copy the Ten Commandments over one hundred times— with parental signature required.

As a chastised fifth-grader, I wasn't very happy about my dubious status as the "lines" record-holder. But I think that even then I had a vague notion that Mr. Dykstra was on firm theological footing when he gave me that particular assignment. And over the years I have come to appreciate his spiritual insight more and more.

In hurling my rude epithet at the young black man, I really was violating God's Law. I was bearing false witness against my neighbor. I wasn't being a truthful person. And God takes truthfulness very seriously.

The Listening God

Civil people watch their language. We must hold ourselves responsible for what we say.

Parents sometimes tell their children that some words are not to be used in "polite company." But we Christians know that we are always in "polite company." We live our lives in the divine presence. No word escapes God's notice. It is never a legitimate excuse for a Christian to say, "I didn't realize that anyone was listening." God is always listening, and some words are so offensive to God that they should never be uttered.

Racist language falls into that category. All human beings are God's handiwork. Each person is a very precious work of divine art. To make light of an artist's work within the artist's earshot is a cruel thing to do. To demean one of God's most precious artworks when God is listening—and he always is—crudely dishonors the divine artist.

As I've said, when I lashed out at the African-American student with the "N" word I was violating God's Law by bearing false witness against my neighbor. But that isn't the only commandment I broke. Mr. Dykstra knew what he was doing when he assigned all ten of the commandments to me. A good Calvinist, he knew the Heidelberg Catechism, which says that the commandment "You shall not kill" means that it is wrong to "dishonor, hate, wound, or kill my neighbor" even when I do so only "in thought" or "in word or gesture." And I broke at least one other commandment: the one against theft. When I used that terrible word, I was attempting to steal some God-given dignity from another human being.

Nurturing Habits of Speech

God is *always* listening to what we say. That can be a rather intimidating thought. It might seem that the best policy is not to say much at all, rather than run the risk of saying the wrong thing.

But that is not what I am recommending. It is not God's desire for us to live in constant anxiety about our speech. It is a good thing, however, to spend some time nurturing good speech habits.

Consider this: People who are skilled at dinner-party etiquette do not nervously worry about every move they make. They have nurtured the appropriate sensitivities. Having done that, they are free to enjoy their meals.

We convicted people need a similar kind of nurturing. Through the centuries of church history, many Christians have been cruel and reckless speakers. Sometimes we have even thought of our uncivil speech as an exercise in Christian virtue. So some of us have some unlearning to do if we are going to enter the public square with confidence, as persons of good manners.

Again, that doesn't mean we must go through our lives constantly worrying about how we talk. The key is to form good habits. And in this case at least, our habits are closely connected to our way of viewing things.

I would not have solved my problem with racist epithets if I had only gotten nervous about using the "N" word. My language problem was rooted in a deeper problem that I had to work through: how I viewed members of other groups. It is clear from the punishment he imposed on me that Mr. Dykstra had a good grasp of the basic problem.

We need to think about how we view other people, about how we live with the fact that there are people around who strongly disagree with us about important matters. Our children's friends come from families that worship strange gods. We work alongside people whose convictions about abortion and sex and wealth are very different from our own. In restaurants and airports we encounter lifestyles that shock our deepest sensibilities. To think carefully about how we ought to handle all of this is an important part of nurturing good speech habits.

Angry Rhetoric

The visit of Yasir Arafat to the United Nations in the mid-1970s was the occasion for some very angry talk in the UN General Assembly. The Israelis denounced the Palestine Liberation Organization as "murderers" and "gangsters." Mr. Arafat's defenders responded with the charge that Israel's "Zionist ideology" reveals "a new facet of Nazism."

In an article published shortly after Arafat's visit, two seasoned UN watchers observed that this rhetorical exchange constituted a low point in UN debate. Indeed, the words that were used were so harmful, they argued, that one can only wonder how the harm could ever really be undone:

Even if, by some unknown chance, the PLO and the Israelis eventually reach the point of talking to one another, the suspicions and hatreds engendered by the vicious insults will be difficult to overcome. Will the PLO be capable of forgiving those who described them as cowardly murderers of children, and will the descendants of Hitler's victims be able to talk peace with those who described them as Nazis?[1]

It would not be a bad idea if the UN General Assembly turned into a massive sensitivity group for a while. If talk about "what I think I hear you saying" or how "I'm feeling threatened right now" could become the officially required language for international discussion, some deeply felt grievances might actually be aired in a way that could promote healing rather than further alienation.

I wish the Christian churches could offer some guidance for this kind of organizational therapy. After all, we are supposed to be a model community in which other people can see how God intends diverse individuals and groups to get along.

Unfortunately, that is not very often how it works. The accusatory rhetoric at the United Nations is not all that different in tone from the way Christians argue with each other. Here is an example from the seventeenth century, when the Puritans and the Quakers were engaged in angry debates: The great Puritan preacher Richard Baxter wrote a pamphlet in which he lumped the Quakers with "drunkards, swearers, whoremongers, and sensual wretches" and other "miserable creatures." And then—just in case he had not yet insulted them enough—he insisted that Quakers are no better than "Papists."

The Quaker leader James Naylor announced that he was compelled "by the Spirit of Jesus Christ" to respond to these harsh accusations. He proceeded to characterize his Puritan opponent as a "Serpent," a "Liar," a "Child of the Devil," a "Cursed Hypocrite," and a "Dumb Dog."[2]

This is strong stuff. What makes it especially sad is that the angry talk often makes it difficult to get to the real issues. The debate between the Puritans and the Quakers was actually a rather interesting and helpful one. Both parties engaged in some serious biblical exposition; if the heavy rhetoric were removed, the discussion could easily appear to have been a friendly argument between Christians who had some important things to talk about. But I doubt that either group heard the helpful things the other side was saying. Too much angry rhetoric was in the air.

In the Israeli-PLO debates, both sides raise significant issues, ones that are not easily resolved—questions about ethnicity and nationhood, religious pluralism, national borders and so on. But they have set up the conversation in such a way that these important matters are extremely difficult to discuss.

Let me be very clear. I am not advocating the naive optimism that says all our problems would go away if only we could learn to communicate better. Taking strong convictions seriously means refusing to romanticize away our serious disagreements. In some cases, when we come to understand better what the other side really means to say we will find out that their viewpoint is even worse than we thought at the outset.

But that is no reason for refusing to make the effort. If we end up disagreeing after all is said and done, then at least our disagreement will be an honest one.

Crusades

Still, some Christians seem to be unmoved by a plea for honest understanding. They don't appear to care whether they are fair in characterizing the views of their opponents.

This attitude is often closely tied to a *crusading* mentality. Crusaders are people who think the cause they are fighting for is so important that they must use all means at their disposal to win. For many of us who subscribe to the "just war" perspective on military questions, the crusader is the most difficult opponent to reason with.

That may come as a surprise. You might assume that the classic moral argument about warfare is between those who think it is never right to use violence (pacifists) and those who think violence is sometimes a permissible means for solving problems (just-war advocates). To be sure, that *is* an important argument. But as John Howard Yoder has pointed out, the argument between pacifists and just-war advocates is at least between people who believe the use of violence is subject to some kind of moral limits. These people end up on the same side when they encounter the crusading perspective, which says that anything goes in a military conflict.[3]

The crusading mentality is not limited to military campaigns. Many Christians are spiritual crusaders. They take a no-holds-barred approach to theological or moral arguments with other people. They are not about to listen carefully to their opponents, and anything goes when it comes to the choice of tactics.

The abortion debate is a good case in point. I believe that an abortion is the taking of a human life, so abortions are always regrettable. But I don't agree with some right-to-lifers that all abortions are murders.

The term *murder* has a technical meaning in the law courts. A murder is different from, say, involuntary or voluntary manslaughter. Appealing to this legal meaning is not quibbling. We have developed our legal terminology in response to the complexities that attend issues of life and death.

The wife who pulls the plug on a husband who has been vegetating in a hospital room for a year has done something regrettable and illegal. But she is not a murderer. She has not wantonly and maliciously set out to take another human life. And I am convinced that the same is true of many persons who are involved in abortions. There may be the occasional one who acts with malicious intent toward the fetus. But that is not generally the case. To say "Abortion is murder" is neither fair nor helpful.

When I raise these issues with some of my right-to-life friends, they usually concede that the word *murder* may be a bit inflated. But some of them insist that it is still a useful term in the debate. We are in a major struggle, they say. We don't have time to stop and think about all the moral niceties.

That's the crusading spirit. Win at all—or almost all—costs. The battle is too important; we can't be inhibited by scruples about whether we are being fair to the enemy. Is the cause an important one or isn't it? If it is important, then let's get on with the battle.

Here we have to try to get the crusaders to face a crucial issue: What *is* the cause? What is the battle *for*? For Christians, the cause must be the glory of God. And then the basic question is: How is God glorified? Is God honored when we play fast and loose with the truth? Is God glorified by our unwillingness to understand other people's intentions before we attack them?

I must confess: I have quite a bit of the crusader in me. But in the next chapter I will attempt to provide a case against crusading Christianity. And I will be arguing with impulses that lurk deep within my own soul.

I do not think I am alone in this. Convicted Christians will often be tempted by the crusading spirit. So a rule of thumb is necessary: *For starters, concentrate on your own sinfulness and on the other person's humanness.* We become more civil by gaining a more honest picture of ourselves and others.

A friend who is active in the right-to-life movement told me a poignant story about a Christian woman who was outspoken in opposing abortion: no compromises, no exceptions. Eventually, however, people noticed that she was no longer showing up at right-to-life events. She had quietly dropped out, with no explanations given.

Later, her friends found out that her fifteen-year-old daughter had become pregnant as a result of an especially brutal rape, and after much agonizing the family had opted for abortion.

I sympathize with that family's decision. There are tragic circumstances in which abortion is the least evil alternative. I can understand why these people felt abortion was their best available—or least horrible—choice.

This Christian woman and mother finally acknowledged the complexity of the abortion question. But why did she have to wait until rape-pregnancy became an intensely personal dilemma before she could be sensitive to the nuances of the abortion debate? Wouldn't it have been better for her to learn sensitivity by cultivating an empathy that extended beyond her immediate family?

To be sure, empathy alone will not solve the issues of abortion policy. But this woman's about-face on the subject suggests that her all-or-nothing rhetoric had been a substitute for an honest wrestling with the issues. She could have been a much more effective proponent for the right-to-life cause if earlier on she had engaged in the exercises prescribed in our rule of thumb: taking a fearless look at her own motives and probing sensitively for her opponents' genuinely human concerns.

Here are a few lines from an evangelical acquaintance in Northern Ireland, who wrote recently to tell me of a proposal he has made to religious leaders in his country:

> One way of assisting the promotion of peace in our society would be to arrange an annual debate between Roman Catholic and Protestant school teams on some topic related to Irish history. My suggested twist was that the Protestant team should argue the case from the Catholic viewpoint and vice versa. It seems to me that the ability to get right into the other person's shoes is sadly lacking in our situation.

Prominent leaders from both sides of the Catholic-Protestant divide have written, my friend says, to support his proposal. "As far as I know, however, nobody has taken the idea any further." My guess is that much could be accomplished if Irish Protestants and Catholics would seriously pursue such an exercise in empathic speaking and listening.

The Divine Gaze

Getting cured of incivility means learning how to speak more honestly. But I have insisted that civility runs deeper than words. It is grounded in the way we view reality. This means that we Christians must work to view things—as far as possible for mere mortals—the way God does.

Psalm 139 is one of my favorite biblical passages. It's filled with awe in the presence of the divine holiness. But it also contains what strikes me as a delightful and instructive little drama. For eighteen marvelous verses the writer extols the mysteries of God's knowledge and power. Then he gets so overwhelmed by this spiritual exercise that he seems to slip into a crusading spirit for a few verses:

Do I not hate those who hate you, O LORD? And do I not loathe those who rise up against you? I hate them with perfect hatred; I count them my enemies. (vv. 21-22)

This is an understandable reaction, and in a sense it is perfectly legitimate. God's majesty is so awesome that everything else pales in comparison. How can we offer anything short of total commitment to such a being? Can we do anything less than hate those who hate the Lord and loathe those who rise up against him?

But abruptly the psalmist seems to catch himself. He senses that it is rather presumptuous for a creature such as he to pretend to have either the knowledge or the integrity to possess a "perfect hatred" of unrighteousness. So he pleads, not for the defeat of the hosts of wicked ones, but for a correcting grace that will reach into the depths of his own being:

Search me, O God, and know my heart;
test me and know my thoughts.
See if there is any wicked way in me,
and lead me in the way everlasting. (vv. 23-24)

This is where a proper view of reality begins: in our own awareness of the divine gaze. The Lord not only hears all—he sees all. He knows not only our habits of speech; he sees the hearts in which those habits are formed. Christian discipleship is permeated by the consciousness that we live *coram Deo*—before the face of God.

There is an inescapably passive dimension to the Christian life. I like the way Gustavo Gutierrez puts it. The Christian life, he says, must include some "useless," "wasted" time for spirituality—periods in which we have no other agenda than to *be* in the divine presence.[4]

Seeing As God Sees

This Christian passivity does have its connections, however, to the more active dimensions of the Christian life. In quiet times when we are intensely conscious of the divine gaze, we learn to act in a way that honors God's perspective on reality. Having been aware of *being seen* by God, we can actively begin to *see* in a more truthful and civil manner.

A few years ago my wife and I joined several missionary families in Haiti for a retreat. One afternoon we drove through the countryside in a Land Rover, and I sat in the back with the missionaries' children. Two of them were beautiful twin Haitian girls who had been adopted after they were abandoned as babies on the missionaries' doorstep.

As we rode along, the children began to sing Sunday-school songs: "Jesus Loves Me," "Jesus Loves the Little Children," "This Little Light of Mine," and so on. I sang along until they started on this song:

O be careful, little eyes, what you see

O be careful, little eyes, what you see

For the Father up above is looking down in love

O be careful, little eyes, what you see.

The verses went on: "O be careful, little ears, what you hear. . . . O be careful, little feet, where you go. . . . O be careful, little tongue, what you say. . . ."

This ditty had always struck me as much too negative: Don't see this. Don't touch this. Don't walk there. And as I listened to it in this Land Rover, I looked out the window and saw some of the most desperate poverty that any human being could experience. Rows and 'rows of shanties unfit for human habitation. Malnourished bodies. Faces marked by despair and hopelessness. The sights and smells of decay and death.

Isn't it ironic? I thought. *Here we are passing through scenes of horrible human degradation, and we are singing a negative little spiritual song about all the things that we ought not to be doing as Christians!*

Then suddenly I realized there is a very different way of understanding that song. I had always interpreted it as a set of "don'ts." But it could just as easily be understood as a series of "do's." Be careful to *see* what God sees. Be careful to *hear* what God hears. Be careful to *go* where God goes. . . .

Then I realized these children were singing about a very active Christianity. These two little Haitian girls had become members of this missionary community precisely *because* that community was willing to see and hear and touch in a God-honoring way.

Civil Christians know that they must actively "be careful" about what they say. But they also connect their ways of speaking to their ways of seeing and hearing and walking and touching. And this in turn means an awareness of the "polite company" whose Presence they can never escape.

5
Open
Hearts

The Importance of Civil Attitudes

• • •

ONE AFTERNOON IN a department store, I watched a little boy tease his sister. When his mother noticed what he was doing, she scolded him and gave him an order: "Start being nice!"

I felt sorry for the boy. Those *be*-something orders are tough ones to obey. If the mother had said, "Stop teasing her!" that would have been a little easier. You know how to obey a command like that: you simply stop doing what you were told not to do. But how do you simply start *being* nice? Niceness takes work. It requires that we cultivate certain attitudes and dispositions. You do not just close your eyes and summon up the will to *be* nice.

Being civil is closely related to being nice. Like "nice," "civil" is not an easy thing simply to *be*. We have to work at it on several fronts.

At the very least, like the boy in the store, we have to stop doing the things that are *not* nice. But we have to work on our inner selves as well. The impulses of civility need to flow from our hearts. We have already touched on some ways to make this happen. In this chapter we will look more closely at ways of opening our hearts to the experiences of people who are different from us.

Empathy

One of the last documents that the Roman Catholic bishops approved during the Second Vatican Council was the "Pastoral Constitution on the Church in the Modern World." In spite of that rather forbidding title, it is a very warm and inspiring document. I find the opening words especially moving:

> The joy and the hope, the grief and anguish of the men of our time, especially of those who are poor or afflicted in any way, are the joy and hope, the grief and anguish of the followers of Christ as well. Nothing that is genuinely human fails to find an echo in their hearts.[1]

This is a powerful call. Civility requires that we reduce the psychological distance between ourselves and others. We need to develop a sense of commonality with people who initially strike us as very different from ourselves. One important means of doing this is by cultivating *empathy*.

"Empathy" literally means "in-feeling"—it is to project myself into another person's feelings so that I begin to understand what it is like to have his experiences. If I want to gain empathy for a neighbor who is consistently defensive and insulting, I can try to imagine what it is like to be torn by the hurts and fears that give rise to his antisocial behavior. In doing so I may find links between his inner life and my own; or I may use my imagination to explore feelings that I myself have never experienced directly.

Obviously, we cannot develop empathy toward each of our fellow-citizens on a one-to-one basis. But we can cultivate empathic sensitivities toward people in general by concentrating on some of our commonalities.

I'm highlighting the need for empathy here because I believe that the enlargement of our empathic sensitivities is an important part of becoming more human. When we break out of the bonds of self-centeredness, entering into the experiences of other people, we come closer to fulfilling God's purposes for human beings. And we become more Christlike, since the incarnation is the ultimate ministry of empathy: "For we do not have a high priest who is unable to sympathize with our weaknesses, but we have one who in every respect has been tested as we are, yet without sin" (Heb 4:15).

Empathy is good for our character development, but that is not its only value. It is also important for our evangelistic efforts. Christian groups that emphasize the need for "relational evangelism" recognize this point. They know that forming genuine friendships with unbelievers—so that we enter into their lives in order to learn about their uniquely individual hopes and fears—establishes a healthy basis for introducing them to the person and work of the Savior.

Curiosity

The quest for empathy can be helped along by a good dose of *curiosity*. We ought to want to become familiar with the experiences of people who are different from us simply out of a desire to understand the length and breadth of what it means to be human.

Curiosity is a motivating force for many good things in our lives. It is at work when we decide to take a continuing education course, or try to figure out how something works, or travel to another country, or go backpacking in unfamiliar territory. Because of curiosity we page through magazines and watch the news and read novels and call our friends to find out "what's new."

Christian people need a strong sense of curiosity. This is God's world, and we ought to want to understand it better. And since human beings are such an important part of the divine scheme—"fearfully and wonderfully made" (Ps 139:14)—we ought to be very curious about the full range of human experience. We want to learn about people who are very different from ourselves.

All of this applies directly to our public lives. We ought to want to know what makes our fellow citizens tick, why they think and act the way they do, how they have formed their deepest loves and loyalties. To learn civility in the public square is one important way to satisfy a healthy curiosity about what is "genuinely human."

Teachability

Civility also requires that we approach others in a spirit of *teachability*. Now, in a sense we have already been talking about cultivating a teachable spirit in our comments on empathy and curiosity. To be empathic and curious in our relations with other people is to want to learn about them.

What I want to emphasize here, though, is not learning *about* them, but learning *from* them. For example, I have read many books and essays both by and about the great nineteenth-century thinker Friedrich Nietzsche. Nietzsche was an outspoken atheist whose philosophical views bordered on nihilism. When he said "God is dead," he was not glibly dismissing revealed religion. He meant to show how we lose our sense of meaning and purpose when we deny God's reality.

I think I have gained some empathy for Nietzsche as I have studied his life and thought. He was a complex man, fascinating in many ways. I have tried to see things from his point of view—to *feel* what it must have been like for him to see the world as he did. In studying him, I have also satisfied my curiosity about his life and thought. I have gained some grasp of the cultural setting in which he came to his positions, and I have learned something about the pattern of his intellectual development.

But there are yet other questions I can ask myself: Did I learn anything *from* Nietzsche? What (if anything) have I gleaned from studying the life and thought of this man who so violently rejected the convictions of his Lutheran forebears?

Have I come to agree with some of his views? This is a different issue, and a more difficult one. I believe that I have profited from my study of Nietzschean philosophy—but I would be hard put to identify a specific idea that he succeeded in *teaching* me.

Here are two important observations about the example I just laid out. First, I am not embarrassed to admit that I cannot think of a specific lesson I learned from Nietzsche. We are not obligated to find some bit of truth in every perspective we encounter. Some points of view are thoroughly confused or distorted; some are even crazy. We have done a good job if we have managed to engage another person's viewpoint with empathy and curiosity.

Second, however, I need not be embarrassed to confess that I *have* learned something from Nietzsche if that has been my experience. Any encounter with an unbeliever may leave me with a better grasp of the truth.

God often instructs believers in unpredictable ways. The prophet Balaam was corrected by words that came from the mouth of his donkey. A group of pagan sailors confronted Jonah with the fact that he was trying to run from the call of God. Every year at Christmas we gain inspiration from a group of Eastern magi who found the Christ-child by consulting their astrological charts.

The Lord often sends strange teachers our way. We need to be open to the lessons he wants us to learn from them.

Learning from Unbelief

There are various kinds of "truths" we can learn from people with whom we disagree on very basic matters. Sometimes we can learn important lessons simply by attending carefully to the stark contrast between our views and those of unbelievers.

I *have* learned from Nietzsche in this way. He insists that our world carries no trace of divine order or goodness. Such a world would be quite horrible to live in, and Nietzsche is aware of that fact. He means to be a very consistent atheist—he does not want to borrow anything from the biblical world view he has rejected. The contrast between his philosophy and the Bible's portrayal of reality is very instructive. Nietzsche has helped us all, believer and unbeliever alike, to define the issues between us in unmistakably clear terms.

Sometimes non-Christians can also help us to see things that we have overlooked in the biblical perspective. For example, I have very little in common with Marxists; in my opinion, the Communist ideology is mostly misguided. But I do sense that Karl Marx's followers are right in showing how Christians have sometimes failed to respond to the plight of the poor and the oppressed.

Learning that lesson from Marxism, however, sends us back to the pages of the Scriptures, where we hear anew God's call for us to take up the cause of the widow, the orphan, the sojourner and the victim of tyranny (see, for example, Ps 146).

And sometimes unbelievers tell us things that are true in a rather straightforward sense. Jesus himself urges us to be open to the possibility that "the children of this age are more shrewd in dealing with their own generation than are the children of light" (Lk 16:8).

We cannot place artificial limits on how God may speak to us. This has relevance to our encounters in the public square. When we approach others in a civil manner, we must listen carefully to them. Even when we strongly disagree with their basic perspectives, we must be open to the possibility that they will help us discern the truth more clearly. Being a civil Christian means being open to God's surprises.

Blurring the Lines?

The well-known Catholic ethicist Charles Curran tells how one day he was on his way to give an exam to his ethics class at the Catholic University. He was walking behind two of his students, who did not know that Father Curran was within earshot.

"Did you study for Curran's test?" one student asked his friend.

"Not too much," the other replied. "With Curran all you have to do is talk a lot about how complex and ambiguous everything is, and you're sure to get a good grade!"

Perhaps readers will gain the same impression from what I am arguing in these pages. I have already said it, and I will say it again: the issues *are* often complex and ambiguous. We have to be open to what our opponents have to tell us. We shouldn't be too quick to reject the other person's point of view.

Isn't this a dangerous line of thought? In making so much of complexity and ambiguity, don't we run the risk of blurring the boundary lines? Isn't all of this talk about empathy and self-examination a luxury that only intellectuals can afford? Think about those people whom we most revere for their moral courage—aren't they actually rather "naive" and "unnuanced" in their convictions?

These points are well taken. Still, I have some of these naive, unnuanced, morally courageous people in mind as I develop my case for civility. Two of my spiritual heroines come quickly to mind. Corrie ten Boom: she was willing to put her own life on the line to protect Jews from the horrors of Nazi persecution— yet she acted in a loving and gentle manner, praying for her enemies even as she worked to thwart their evil designs. And Mother Teresa: while she is an unyielding foe of abortion-on-demand, the kindness and reverence of her humble spirit is always obvious.

Such moral "simplicity" seems to come into some lives with little visible effort. Others of us, though, must expend much spiritual and intellectual energy in order to take even a few modest steps in the direction of this kind of sainthood.

To be sure, insisting on ambiguity and complexity can be a tactic for avoiding necessary moral struggles. But, when accompanied by a genuine openness to God's corrective grace in our lives, it can also be a means of sanctification.

We keep coming back to this point: we live in the presence of God. We cannot consistently develop empathy and curiosity and teachability in our relationships without the reinforcing experiences of divine grace. We can sustain open hearts toward others only because of the love that flows from the heart of God.

6
What's Good
About
Pluralism?

• • •

CHRISTIAN HEARTS must be open to other people because
God has opened his heart to us. That is what I have just been
arguing. But just how open are we supposed to *be*? We live
today in the midst of many lifestyles, many systems of
thought—don't we run the risk of having our hearts pulled in
so many different directions that we will finally have no center
of our own?

That is an important concern. There is much about contemporary pluralism that frightens me. But there is also much that
I find exciting from a Christian point of view.

Someone said to me recently: "I can't imagine a more urgent
topic than the subject of pluralism. We Christians need all the

help we can get in learning to cope with our pluralistic society."

I almost challenged his choice of the word *cope*, but then I thought better of it. I have a pretty good idea why he used it. He was thinking of all the strange things that go on around us—these days it seems that no idea or practice is too far out to attract a glowing endorsement from some celebrity. The diversity of world views and lifestyles we encounter on a regular basis can be very bewildering. And when one is genuinely bewildered, being able to "cope" is the most one can hope for.

But pluralism is a slippery concept. It gets used in a number of different ways by people who analyze contemporary society. And not everything that is called "pluralistic" is necessarily bad from a Christian point of view.

Pluralism is "many-ism." When we use the word, we are pointing to some sort of diversity. How we are to react to that diversity depends on what kind of "many-ness" we are singling out for attention. In some cases, pluralism isn't just something to cope with—it is a thing to be celebrated.

God and Diversity

At a meeting of theologians the conversation somehow got around to the question of life on other planets. This is not a subject that I have ever taken very seriously, so I was surprised when a respected theologian spoke enthusiastically about the possibility of intelligent life in other parts of the universe. When I questioned him further, his response was a thoughtful one: "I believe that God has an infinite imagination, don't you? And if that is so, why should we assume that God would want to limit the creation to what we see around us?" That argument is worth pondering. And we can also apply it to the question of diversity within our own world. God has already demonstrated a rich imagination, simply by producing the creatures we see around us.

The South African politician Nic Diederichs once made a rather provocative observation: God, he said, dislikes deadly uniformity. I hate to admit that I like that comment, since Diederichs was a perverse thinker who helped to create the apartheid ideology in South Africa. Defending the "separate development" of the races, he argued that God wills the existence of many different races; that is why we must not allow interracial mingling. What God has put asunder, let no one try to join together![1]

The ugliness of Diederichs's intentions ought not to blind us to the truth of his theological premise. The God of the Bible *does* seem to dislike deadly uniformity. Whenever I read the creation account in Genesis 1, for example, I am taken with the delight that God expresses as he calls the world's rich diversity into existence. God's mood seems positively playful as he anticipates all that "multiplication": "Let the waters bring forth swarms of living creatures!" "Be fruitful and multiply and fill the waters in the seas, and let birds multiply on the earth!" "Let the earth bring forth living creatures of every kind!" (Gen 1:20, 22, 24).

God has an infinite imagination. He loves diversity. And because of this, no Christian can oppose diversity as such. There are certain kinds of "swarms" in which God takes delight.

To say that we live in a pluralistic culture is simply to say that we are surrounded by plurality. And again: many-ness itself is not a bad thing.

But neither is many-ness necessarily a *good* thing. This is where Nic Diederichs went wrong. Having pointed to God's love of diversity, he tries to sneak over on us the wrongheaded notion that God hates to see the mixing and combining of diverse races.

We have to be discerning in our endorsement of many-ness. Some pluralities are pleasing to God, but others are not. God takes delight in the diversity of animal life—better many different kinds of animal than one dull, uniform species. But, on the other hand, God does not take delight in the existence of many different kinds of diseases, or many forms of human perversity. The fallen world "swarms" with many things that do not please him.

The Pluralistic Consciousness

There have always been many "swarms" in the world. In that sense, coping with many-ness is not a new experience. But it is also true that we are experiencing pluralism in new ways these days. Many scholars insist that a pluralistic consciousness is one of the unique characteristics of contemporary life.

What is it that makes our present-day encounter with pluralism so special? It is the fact that we are immersed in *a culture of options.*

Think of someone who lived in Western Europe during the Middle Ages. As the daughter of a peasant Christian family, she had few real choices about how she would live her life. She would marry and bear children—the only alternative would be to join a religious order. She would never travel more than twenty miles from the house where she was born. It was unthinkable that she would ever enjoy the luxuries known to the wealthy. Whatever her private opinions or attitudes about religious matters, she would attend church regularly—and there was no question about which church it would be, since there were no alternatives.

Choosing what she would be never occurred to such a person.

She was locked into her station in life.

By the time of the Reformation, things had begun to change. One obvious difference was that more and more people were faced with the choice of what form of religion (or nonreligion) to embrace. Geographical mobility was on the increase. Some folks were even able to move from one economic class to another. New trades and professions meant that for many people the question of vocation became a matter of conscious deliberation.

Today's range of choices is so great, though, that quantitative terms alone are not adequate to describe the change that has taken place. Choosing has become a way of life. Do I want to continue in my present profession or go into something completely different? In which state shall I live—or should I try another country? What part of the world shall I visit next? What do I want my next spouse to be like? Which religion best serves my present needs?

Immersion in a world of seemingly infinite options—this is the pluralistic consciousness. And our unique awareness of a plurality of alternatives is not a totally bad thing. We may not like the fact that everything seems to be up for grabs these days. But we certainly want to preserve our range of choices about what we most treasure. Whenever we Christians celebrate our freedom to worship God as we please and to live our lives in the light of our deepest convictions, we are actually rejoicing over our uniquely pluralistic consciousness.

Pluralism and Idolatry

When someone refers to "our pluralistic society," then, we need to find out what is meant before we can respond properly. The fact is, the phrase is used in a number of different ways. We cannot sort out all the meanings here.[2] But it will help to think briefly about how Christians should evaluate two very prevalent forms of pluralism.

The first form is what our "coping" person has in mind. He is bewildered by the "swarm" of *world views and value systems* that he sees around him: he hears a babble of voices proclaiming the merits of a stunning array of philosophies and ideologies and religions. Buddhism. Islam. Jehovah's Witnesses. Radical feminism. Deconstructionism. The occult. New Age. Liberalism. Conservatism. Neoconservatism. It is understandable that a person could be dismayed by all of this.

What about God? Is the Creator also disturbed by this kind of pluralism? If we take the Bible seriously, then we really have no choice but to say that he is—that God doesn't like this kind of diversity. The reason for God's disapproval was laid out earlier in our discussion of the causes of incivility. God disapproves of the pluralism of *idolatries.*

Each world view or value system sets forth a picture of what reality and goodness are all about. And even though we are being presented with myriad choices these days, the basic issue is still simple: either your view of reality and goodness is God-centered, as laid out in the Bible, or it is not.

If your picture has the biblical God at the center of things, it is an accurate one. If it places something or someone else at the center, it is idolatrous. Those are the fundamental alternatives as defined by the Scriptures.

This does not mean that idolaters have nothing to teach us— we have already discussed this, and we will be coming back to the subject. Nor does it mean that we should use political means to try to wipe out the pluralism of idolatries. The most effective way of opposing falsehood is *witnessing to the power of truth.*

A thoroughly democratic society, in which people are granted the right to live out their basic commitments, provides us with an excellent arena for Christian evangelism and teaching. If diverse viewpoints have a right to be expressed, then ours has a right to be expressed. It is to our advantage, then, to promote a political system that encourages religious pluralism.

Cultural Diversity

Sometimes people have another kind of "swarm" in mind when they talk about "our pluralistic society." They are pointing not to the plurality of world views and value systems, but to the diversity of what I will call, for lack of a better term, *cultural perspectives*. What is at stake here is not so much diverse *views* of reality as diverse *viewings* of the world. We all stand in a cultural "place"; our outlooks are shaped by such factors as ethnicity, race, geography, language, economic status and gender.

These things do influence the way we interpret reality. But it would be misleading to evaluate these differences as matters of truth and goodness. Being a Swedish-American rural woman from Minnesota doesn't "weigh" more or less on the scales of truth and goodness than being an African-American inner-city man from Memphis. Questions of truth and goodness come in only at the world view level. I begin to get an idea how to start "weighing" when I find out, for example, that the woman from Minnesota edits the local newsletter for "freethinkers," while the man from Memphis runs a Baptist mission for the homeless.

Of course, anything can become an idol—including race, gender and economic status. But none of these things is "naturally" an idol.

I have a theological hunch about the diversity of cultural perspectives. I think that many of these differences were a part of God's good plan from the beginning. That gender was there at the start is obvious: "male and female he created them" (Gen 1:27). But I suspect God had some of the other things in mind as well—the diversity of race, ethnicity and geographic temperament.

Some theologians have made this notion part of the very idea of "the image of God." Not only is each human being created in the divine image, they argue, but the human race as a whole also has the image of God in a *collective* sense—so that the rich diversity of cultures on the face of the earth shows forth the splendor of God in a way that no individual or group does alone.

I like that idea. But whatever we do with it as a theory about our created natures, there can be no question about what God thinks of cultural diversity when it comes to redemption.

Through the atoning blood of Jesus Christ, God is putting together a new kind of human community. "You are a chosen race, a royal priesthood, a holy nation. . . . Once you were not a people, but now you are God's people" (1 Pet 2:9-10). And the building blocks of this new community are the diverse cultural groupings that we see in the world.

To be sure, cultural pluralism in our present sinful world is seldom separate from other kinds of pluralism. Cultural diversity is regularly intertwined, for example, with a diversity of world views and value systems.

But because the richness of human diversity is precious in the sight of God, we have to work hard at doing the disentangling. Learning to appreciate cultural differences in the light of biblical revelation is an important and necessary part of our maturation in Christ. This appreciation is also central to the evangelistic task—we must bring the gospel to people in different cultures without destroying cultural diversity.

So there is at least one kind of pluralism that God loves. God cares deeply about cultural diversity. This means that Christians need not be threatened by cultural differences as such. These differences are to be sanctified, not eradicated. *This* kind of pluralism—an appreciation for the contribution each cultural group makes to the beauty of the divine mosaic—inspires the heavenly choirs to break forth with a song of joyful praise to the Lamb:

> You are worthy to take the scroll
> > and to open its seals,
> for you were slaughtered and by your blood you ransomed
> > for God
> > saints from every tribe and language and people
> > and nation;
> you have made them to be a kingdom and priests serving
> > our God,
> > and they will reign on earth. (Rev 5:9-10)

We cannot be any less affirming in our own—more earthly—encounters with created human diversity. To cultivate that spirit of affirmation is crucial to our growth in civility. It is also a good way to get ready for heaven!

7
How to Be Civil About Sex

• • •

CIVILITY IS HARDER in some contexts than in others, depending on what is at stake. How can I be civil to someone who is making bad sexual choices—abortion, homosexuality, promiscuity? What about dealing with my new Muslim neighbors? And isn't it impossible to work in the television industry without being tarnished by evil?

We need to focus on some of the more complicated areas. In chapters eight and nine we'll think about religious diversity and about leadership in a pluralistic society. In this chapter, we will look at the challenges of being civil about sexuality.

The Importance of Sex
"What's with you evangelical types? You seem to be obsessed

with people's sex lives. Pornography, homosexuality, abortion, divorce, fornication, adultery—these are the only social issues you seem to get excited about. Can't you find more interesting things to do than constantly trying to regulate everybody's sexual and reproductive functions?"

I hear this complaint often. And I am quick to acknowledge that there is a grain of truth in it. The social concerns of evangelical Protestants—and other conservative religious groups such as Roman Catholics, Mormons and Orthodox Jews—do seem to focus rather intensely on sex and reproduction. We often give the impression that we do not care nearly as much about racial injustice or economic oppression or environmental exploitation. And that is unfortunate.

But I am not ready to concede that our intense interest in sexual matters is simply misguided. Sexuality is a very important feature of our created nature. The Bible makes this clear in its opening pages: God's first words to the man and woman are "Be fruitful and multiply" (Gen 1:28). And the very first thing that happens to Adam and Eve after they eat the forbidden fruit is that they notice their nakedness and try to cover themselves.

Sex and reproduction play a basic role in the human drama. We humans are complex and vulnerable beings, and our complexity and vulnerability are nowhere more obvious than in our sexuality. A society that is fundamentally confused about the rights and wrongs of sex cannot be very healthy. Public leaders who have casual attitudes toward sexual fidelity will not be trustworthy in other areas of responsibility. Children who have not experienced strong and reliable family bonds are not likely to grow up to be strong and reliable citizens.

That is the way I see things. And if the result is that some people accuse me of worrying too much about sex—well, I will simply have to live with that complaint. Given my strong convictions on the subject, it really is rather difficult for me to be civil about sex.

Difficult—but not impossible. I can work at greater sexual civility without sacrificing my convictions about this crucial dimension of human existence. And I believe it *is* very important to work at this. We convicted Christians may be right to think that sexual values are important to the health of a society. But that does not mean we have done a good job of making our case. The fact is, our record is a poor one.

"Normal" Sexuality?

Several years ago I sat through a debate about homosexuality at a denominational assembly. One minister stood up to tell everyone how strongly opposed he was to homosexual practice. Here is how he put his case: "We normal people should tell these homosexuals that what they are doing is simply an abomination in the eyes of God."

Even though I basically agreed with this pastor's interpretation of biblical teaching, I was very distressed by his speech. I felt like standing up and asking him how "normal" he really was as a sexual being. I thought of another minister, a godly man who was nearing retirement, with whom I had talked recently. Commenting on a younger colleague who had been caught in an adulterous relationship, he had said, "I have no business feeling self-righteous. If my own sexual history were made public, there would be no major scandals. Nothing to get me defrocked. But I would still be ashamed—*so* ashamed!"

I suspect that many of us can identify with that self-assessment. We don't feel very "normal" in our sexuality. The Bible tells us why this is so: we are living in a time of fallenness, of human abnormality. And since sex is central to our nature, our sexuality shows this abnormality in a special way.

We fallen creatures do not like to admit our awareness of our abnormality, so we invent vocabularies to disguise it. Take our labeling system for designating sexual orientations: some people are "gay," we say, and others are "straight." Each of these labels is deceptive. The word *gay* gives the impression that practicing homosexuals are enjoying a happy, carefree way of life. But that is hardly the way it is in a time when the AIDS crisis has brought fear and pain and grief into the lives of so many homosexual persons.

Nor is *straight* a very helpful term. I am not a homosexual—but neither do I feel very "straight" as a human being. I am a fallen creature—bent, crooked, broken. This bentness affects all of my life, including my sexuality.

Homosexuals are not necessarily gay. And the rest of us are not necessarily straight. We are all broken and crooked people. Christians should not be embarrassed to admit this. Most of us have not yet been transformed into fully "normal" people, but we are on the way to normalcy—when Jesus returns "we will be like him, for we will see him as he is" (1 Jn 3:2). In the meantime, we know what to do about our sexual brokenness. We go to the cross and plead for mercy and healing. This experience gives us the message that we can present to other sexual sinners: Join us at the cross!

Guidelines for Sexual Civility
Sexual civility takes effort. It is something we have to work at. Here are some guidelines that can help us along in that process.

Be sexually self-critical. Most of us have no right to set ourselves up as models of sexual "normalcy."

I know it's risky to emphasize this point. Many Christian people are only too aware of their sexual bentness. We have all heard stories of people whose lives are pervaded by sexual guilt and shame. Isn't it very dangerous, then, to insist that we keep a careful eye on our own sexual sins?

The answer, of course, is that it is indeed dangerous. But it's also dangerous to encourage Christians *not* to worry about such matters. A guilty obsession with sexual sin is an unhealthy thing. But it's also unhealthy to think that we should never feel guilty about anything that has to do with sex.

What we need is an honest perspective on our own sexuality. That is what Jesus preached to the sexual hypocrites who wanted to punish the adulterous woman: "Let anyone among you who is without sin be the first to throw a stone at her" (Jn 8:7).

Avoid oversimplifications. Many Christians employ very simple categories in dealing with sexual issues. Here is an example from a well-known fundamentalist preacher's treatment of homosexuality: "My Bible tells me that God created Adam and Eve and not Adam and Steve."

To be sure, this one-liner carries a legitimate point. With the preacher, I believe that the Creator intended genital intimacy to take place within the bonds of heterosexual marriage. But little is to be gained by couching this profound teaching in taunting language.

Remember our own collective sexual sins. Some say that the use of the words *fag* and *faggot* for homosexuals comes from a medieval practice of rounding up known or suspected homosexuals to use them as fuel—as fagots, mere bundles of sticks, as it were—to start village bonfires. I don't know whether this is true, but it may well be. Christians have, in the past, been cruel, unspeakably cruel, to homosexual persons. And that is a very bad thing.

We Christians seem to go through epidemics of serious moral amnesia. We argue about important issues with no memory of the past. Many Christians who disparage feminism seem to have no awareness of how horribly women have often been treated in the Christian community. Christian leaders argue for a separate-but-equal arrangement for the sexes, as if this had always been the viewpoint of the Christian community. But women have regularly been depicted as being inferior to men. Many of them have been severely abused by their Christian fathers and husbands. We have long denied Christian women the right to develop and use God-given gifts—even where the exercise of such gifts has had nothing to do with "headship" patterns.

People are very free these days in talking about their sex lives. Much of this talk makes me nervous. Some of it strikes me as yet another form of promiscuity; it's now permissible to speak very publicly about the most intimate details of our sexuality. But not all sexual candor is bad. It is a good thing to be frank about our sexual sinfulness, both as individuals and as a community with a long history of sexual oppression.

Christians should approach discussions of such topics as homosexuality and feminism in a spirit of sorrow and repentance over our past behaviors and attitudes. No believer need fear that a humble confession of sin will be used to promote the devil's cause. We know that God meets us in our helplessness and honors the sincere acknowledgment of our guilt. We must approach discussions of sexuality, then, with an awareness of the sins we have committed *as* sexual beings and *against* other sexual beings.

Curtail irrational fears. Sometimes our sexual incivilities are grounded in irrationality. We must work at minimizing the degree to which our genuine disagreements with other people get entangled with an irrational fear of "otherness."

Of course, not every criticism of a specific sexual lifestyle should be dismissed as irrational. For example, some of the current talk about "homophobia" is misleading. My disagreement with someone else's view of reality does not mean that I am gripped by a "phobia."

Consider a parallel case: I have strong objections to the dogmas of Mormonism. I'm convinced that many Mormon beliefs and practices are misguided. But I don't think I have a phobia about Mormonism. I have met Mormons whom I like very much—I enjoy talking to them when I sit next to them on planes, and I often have stimulating discussions with Mormon intellectuals. I'm not at all upset at the thought of having Mormon neighbors.

But I do know Christians who have a kind of phobia about the Mormon religion. They talk and act as if Mormons were a special embodiment of evil. They are incapable of having a relaxed conversation with a Mormon. Sometimes they seem to me to be caught up in active hatred of Mormonism.

I have the same feeling about the way many of my Christian friends view homosexuality. Homosexuals represent a despicable "other" in their minds. They have difficulty thinking clearly about the subject. "Homophobia" seems an appropriate label for the attitudes of these Christians.

The alternative is not to uncritically accept active homosexuality. It is important to distinguish between beliefs and behaviors with which we disagree and the very real human beings who believe and behave in those ways. We need to be very clear about our disagreements without responding irrationally to homosexual persons.

Cultivate sexual empathy. A few years ago I attended an "AIDS mass" at a local church. Realizing that the congregation would be made up mostly of persons from the homosexual community in Southern California, I went with the intention of slipping into a back pew to witness the service as an interested onlooker. When I arrived at the church, though, most of the seats were taken. I had to make a split-second choice: either be ushered to an empty spot in the very center of the gathered throng or turn around and head home. I chose to stay.

It was impossible to maintain an aloof, "detached-observer" attitude. The service began with one of my favorite hymns. Then we all prayed together, using these lines from Psalm 139:

For it was you who formed my inward parts;
you knit me together in my mother's womb.
I praise you, for I am fearfully and wonderfully made.
Wonderful are your works;
that I know very well.
My frame was not hidden from you,
when I was being made in secret,
intricately woven in the depths of the earth.
Your eyes beheld my unformed substance. (vv. 13-16)

The mass was a moving experience for me. My views about homosexual practice did not change as a result. But I did come away with a new sense of my similarity to the men and women at that gathering. I had been reminded of a very important lesson: that these were people who, like me, were lovingly fashioned in God's image. The distance of "otherness" between us had been reduced. I gained a new empathy for people whose sexual values are very different from my own.

Sexuality in the Public Square

Following these guidelines would lead us to develop a more civil *attitude* about sexuality. But what are the implications for questions of public policy? How do we deal with controversies about sex in the schools, the arts and the media?

One of my favorite teachers in college, a brilliant English professor, was convinced that Christians should be very reluctant to read literature that contained profanity and explicit sex. One day I challenged her views in a class discussion: "Isn't it important for us to read this kind of thing so that we can at least have a better understanding of what sin is all about?"

I can still hear her stern response: "Mr. Mouw, one doesn't have to smell every garbage can in town in order to know what garbage is!"

In spite of my great respect for her, I did think she was a bit of a prude on this subject. But in the midst of the bombardment of today's sexual culture, I must admit that I have gained some sympathy for her views.

As civil Christians, what ought we to do about increasing displays of promiscuity? How should we position ourselves, for example, in the debates that often rage over "obscene" art and attempts to ban books?

We certainly have a clear right to be strict about such matters *within* the Christian community. Christians are bound together by an explicit covenant of faithful love toward God and neighbor. Departures from this commitment—such as marital infidelity and other kinds of sexual impurity—must be considered serious breaches of faith. The Christian church has rightly included a concern for sexual behavior among its disciplinary ministries. I will be the first to argue strenuously for strong discipline when questions of the church's internal patterns of behavior and attitude are being debated.

But what should be the Christian community's posture toward those who do not acknowledge biblical norms for sexuality? More specifically, in what ways should Christians try to influence the sexual attitudes of those who are not Christian?

Well, let's begin with the obvious. At the very least, Christians ought to *regret* the existence of widespread sexual promiscuity. We know that sexuality has important connections to other significant dimensions of human interaction, and that when people fail to sustain sexual fidelity, the society will have serious problems with commitment and trust. Such a society will inevitably be plagued by other sorts of problems as well.

But we cannot stop at feeling sorry about these patterns. We must also attempt to provide a corrective—by bearing witness to a better way, through scholarship, preaching and evangelism. Exposing the assumptions and implications of sexual anarchy, we can proclaim good news to people whose lives are sexually broken.

What about legislation that would make it more difficult for people to follow through on some of their sinful sexual impulses? I am wary of efforts to establish laws whose primary purpose is to force non-Christians to conform to Christian sexual norms. While it makes sense to construct legislative "fences" around certain practices of sexual exploitation, laws designed to make non-Christians conform grudgingly to Christian rules are not very satisfactory. The Scriptures call human beings to offer God their free obedience. When they choose not to do so, we must respect their choices even if we find them regrettable.

This pattern of respect is exhibited by God himself. When Adam and Eve sinned, God did not destroy them, nor did the Creator try to force their grudging obedience to divine will. Having made their choice, they were free to pursue its implications. Of course, God pointed to the inevitable consequences of their actions. God even locked them out of the Garden because they had rejected its requirements of citizenship. Ultimately, God's rebellious creatures must face the real possibility that utter loneliness and alienation are logical outcomes of their freely chosen path.

It is a dangerous thing for Christians to exercise coercion where even God has refused to force people to do the right thing. So our attempts to promote Christian sexual standards must not be manipulative. There is no value in restricting behavior just because it is sinful behavior.

What, then, *is* it proper for Christians to try to accomplish in the legislative arena? For one thing, we can explore the ways in which public promiscuity does infringe on the legitimate rights of other citizens. It makes good sense, for example, to impose some restrictions on access to certain forms of promiscuous entertainment. In a pluralistic society, people can produce pornographic movies and literature. But that does not mean they are free to run explicit advertisements for their wares on the pages of the daily newspaper. Nor should our children be confronted with racks of sexually explicit books and magazines when they buy their candy bars at the convenience store down the street. We have no automatic right to keep other people from sinning—but neither are we obligated to make it *easy* for them to pursue their warped designs.

Christians can also make a concerted effort to present healthy alternatives to the rebellious idolatries and confusions of contemporary society. We must become more aggressive in demanding a fair trade-off for our willingness to allow others to pursue their preferred lifestyles. If, for example, our society becomes more and more immersed in objectionable values, we must demand the right to educate our children as we see fit without experiencing harassment or unjust financial burdens in the process.

Promoting Sexual Honesty

The "sexual revolution" of the 1960s and 1970s promised us risk-free promiscuity. It should seem obvious by now that the revolution is over. First came widespread venereal disease, and after that the AIDS epidemic. University health clinics have reported increasing numbers of cases of sexual impotence and frigidity among students. There are even thoroughgoing secularists who are now promoting a celibate lifestyle as more "meaningful" than active sexuality. The one theme of the sexual revolution that we Christians should not allow to fade away, though, is *sexual honesty*. None of us, whether believer or unbeliever, can afford to skimp on this commodity.

For many people, of course, sexual honesty has meant that everyone else needs to hear about their "joy of sex" experiences. We need to insist, however, that sexual honesty actually means willingness to engage in patient, nonarrogant discussion of what part sexuality plays in the human condition.

We Christians have to work to overcome the long-standing impression that our message about human sexuality is primarily negative—that we want to keep people from doing enjoyable things. Of course, some Christians have actually *meant* to give that impression. But their negative attitudes miss the heart of the Bible's portrayal of our sexual nature.

The Christian perspective exposes the lie that anything is permissible in our sex lives, just as long as people don't exploit each other. The Bible recognizes that our capacity for exploiting, and for being exploited, is a very deep and subtle thing—too deep to be captured by simple-minded formulas about what is agreeable to "consenting adults." We are vulnerable creatures who easily become confused and misguided in such matters. We need boundaries and reference points to help us to make our way through the most intimate human relationships.

I once had a troubling encounter with a young woman who had been my student at a Christian college. Rebelling against her Christian upbringing, she was now living with a man to whom she was not married. She boasted to me of her new experience of "liberation," now that she had let go of the Christian "guilt trip." I told her that I was very sad about what she was telling me, but that I hoped we could talk more about the subject sometime.

A few months later, she called me to set up an appointment. This time her mood was very different. She had learned that her lover was sexually involved with someone else. When she confronted him, he had accused her of being too "possessive" and had moved on to his new relationship.

My young friend was now experiencing some feelings that do not fit very well in a "liberated" lifestyle. "I feel deeply betrayed," she said through her tears. "He tells me I have been too 'possessive'—well, I think the problem is that I *trusted* him!"

She had been exploited in the name of sexual freedom. Her reaction was precisely the one the Bible says people *ought* to experience when a lover has been unfaithful—a sense of betrayal over the breaking of the most intimate trust that one human being can offer another.

My problem with promiscuous people is not that I think they're having too much fun. Instead, I worry that they must be very unhappy. I want them to flourish as human beings, but they are caught up in a way of life that keeps them from flourishing.

The Bible tells us that we cannot really flourish without working hard at developing our capacity for trust. This is why the Bible places such a strong emphasis on *covenant*. To enter into a covenant is to form a commitment based on trust. When God insisted that Adam and Eve not eat the fruit of one of the trees in the Garden, he was asking them to keep covenant with him. "Trust me," he was saying; "I know what is best for you."

The "trust me" part is crucial to the story. It was here that the Serpent attacked God's credibility. "Did God say *that*?" he asked Eve. "Don't believe God—he just wants to show you who's boss!" When our first parents failed to trust God, they got us all into deep trouble. Trust and commitment are basic to who we are as human beings.

When we don't have a healthy trust in God, it's hard to trust anyone else. God's revealed guidelines for sexuality are meant to create new possibilities for a trusting intimacy.

The whole point of the biblical perspective is to promote a sexuality that is kind and reverent. So it's important that we present the biblical viewpoint kindly and reverently to those with whom we disagree about sexual standards. Not to do so is to undermine our own message. Sexual civility is an important way of living out our commitment to the gospel.

Grace for the Journey
To be sure, cultivating sexual civility is risky. We live in mor-

ally dangerous times. But as we rightly worry about sexual permissiveness, we must not forget the danger of sexual arrogance.

We Christians have no business being arrogant about sexual matters. God is still working at making us into the kind of people he wants us to be; we are on a journey toward wholeness. We need to admit our own vulnerability and be honest about our desperate need for God's grace.

A few years ago, Herbert Chilstrom, head of the Evangelical Lutheran Church in America, wrote a pastoral letter to the clergy of his denomination on the subject of homosexuality. Bishop Chilstrom reiterated the church's opposition to homosexual practice, but he also called on Lutherans to deal with homosexuality in pastorally sensitive ways.

Chilstrom's treatment of the topic had both theological and practical value. One of his illustrations, though, made a special impression on me. He told of a letter he had received from a Scandinavian-American woman. Chilstrom knew her to be a godly person—"a woman of prayer and deep spirituality."

Now in her seventies, this woman had struggled all her life with strong lesbian inclinations. All her efforts to change her orientation had failed. This is what she wrote to Bishop Chilstrom:

All my adult life I have longed for someone special whose hand I could hold, someone . . . I could embrace. When I have encountered the cruelty of . . . the anti-gay expectations, I have wished for a loving shoulder on which I could lean and cry my heart out. But the church doesn't allow for that. I have sometimes thought that when I get to heaven I would like to be held in the Lord's arms for a *long time* to make up for what I have been denied. A lifetime is a long time to wait for something we crave as much as love.

I think of this woman often. She has a prominent place in my gallery of saints. When I think of the mindless comments about homosexuality she has had to endure over the years, I feel very sad. When I reflect on her perseverance in the faith and her longing for the Lord's embrace, I receive strength for my own journey. I hope that when I reach heaven I can hug her. She has helped me much in the task of becoming gentler and more reverent in my attitudes toward sexuality.

8
The Challenge
of Other
Religions

•   •   •

A FEW SUMMERS ago, I spent six weeks doing research in
the Netherlands. I rented some rooms in an old farmhouse on
the edge of a small village, where I did much of my reading and
writing. My great-grandparents emigrated from the Netherlands over a century ago, and sometimes I felt as if I'd been
granted the privilege of traveling back in time to the world they
had known.

From my window I watched old farmers in wooden shoes
walking out to the field to check the sheep and the cows. Wom-
en cycled past on their daily rounds to the bakery, the cheese
store and the greengrocer. Lined along the river bank across the

road were centuries-old houses with newly thatched roofs. In the village there were two churches, both Reformed; the larger town three miles down the road also had two Reformed churches, plus a Catholic one.

Reality intruded quickly into my time-travel reveries, however, when I went out to walk each evening. The sheep yard and barn a few hundred yards down the road fit nicely into the whole scenario—except for the sign that proclaimed the presence of an "Islamic Slaughterhouse," where Turkish immigrants prepared meat in conformity with Muslim dietary regulations.

"World religions" had come to that little Dutch village. And they have also come in full force to the villages and cities of North America. When I was a child, my family prayed regularly for the people "out on the foreign mission field." Today the foreign mission field is just down the road! We can encounter Muslims and Hindus and Buddhists and animists on our evening strolls.

"Knowing" a Religion

How should we respond to these diverse religious perspectives? Do they bring opportunities that we should take advantage of?

Ari Goldman went to Harvard Divinity School to find answers to these questions. Goldman is a religion reporter for *The New York Times.* He is also an Orthodox Jew. In his engaging book *The Search for God at Harvard,* Goldman tells about the sabbatical leave he took in 1985 to study various religious perspectives at Harvard.

Goldman was thrown off-guard when Professor Diana Eck started her first World Religions lecture with this declaration: "If you know one religion . . . you don't know any." Goldman had gone to Harvard thinking that he already knew one religion very well; he had been steeped in the teachings and traditions of Judaism. But Eck's statement made a deep impression on him; he quotes it several times in his book. Clearly, he believes the time he spent studying other religions deepened his understanding of Orthodox Judaism.

I thoroughly enjoyed reading Goldman's book, but I am not quite as taken with Professor Eck's declaration as he is. Indeed, my initial reaction was to reject her comment as a piece of intellectual arrogance. What can it possibly mean to say that one can "know" one religion only after one has studied many of them?

I know dozens of devout Christians who have never given any thought to the content of another religion—does this mean that they do not really "know" Christianity? Could anyone seriously think that some undergraduates who have finished a few courses in comparative religions "know" their own religious perspective better than simple, illiterate folks who have spent their lifetimes worshiping and serving God?

That was my instinctive response to Eck's declaration—and, after reflection, I still think it's a plausible reaction to her statement as it stands. Christian faith, properly understood, is a relationship to God. To know Christianity from the inside is to pray to God, and to read God's Word, and to worship with other people who have come to know God through Jesus Christ. I don't see how taking a course in Buddhism or animism could add anything to this foundational "knowing" of God. Saying "If you know one religion . . . you don't know any" seems to me as confused as saying, "If you know one set of parents . . . you don't know any."

But let me try to be a little more charitable toward Professor

Eck, by following through on my parenting analogy. While it surely would be arrogant to say that you don't really know your parents *at all* until you have compared them carefully to other parents, there is something to be said for exposure to what we might call "comparative parenting."

Actually, it's a very good thing that some experts study parents to understand the differences and similarities in the way parents and offspring relate to each other. These parenting studies often help ordinary people gain a healthier understanding of their own parent-child relationships. New parents find it very helpful to read parenting guides, which are based on studies of many different family settings. Adults who were abused by their parents need desperately to be reassured, by people who know about families in general, that what they experienced was not "normal"—that they don't have to feel guilty about the childhood hurts and fears that still keep cropping up in their lives. And for other people, it is encouraging simply to see that their experiences with parenthood are better than the run-of-the-mill. "Comparative parenting" exercises, then, *can* sometimes help us gain a better grasp of our own very personal parenting relationships. And the same holds for religion. It is surely too simplistic to say, "If you know one religion . . . you don't know any." But it does make sense to say that exposure to other religions can deepen my understanding of my own faith commitment.

Polarized Approaches

We Christians seem to be fond of polarizations. This propensity shows up in discussions about our approach to other religions. Some Christians emphasize evangelizing strategies that are heavily weighted toward explicit convictedness: present the message of the gospel and invite people to become Christians. Other Christians rely heavily on civility: engage in polite dialog with people from other religious communities in the hope of promoting mutual understanding and cooperation.

The defenders of each of these approaches often don't get along very well. The evangelizers accuse the dialoguers of sacrificing the gospel for religious relativism; they fear that the unique claims of Christianity will be bartered away in interreligious dialog. The dialoguers respond by accusing the evangelizers of a religious imperialism that runs roughshod over the genuine insights that can be found in other religious traditions; they want to avoid a dogmatic spirit.

Do these two approaches *need* to be treated as an either-or choice? Is it possible to see evangelism and dialog as complementary activities? I'm inclined to look for some way of integrating the two emphases. Why can't Christians engage in evangelization while at the same time hoping to gain new understanding through dialog with other religions?

When "evangelism" and "dialog" become the watchwords of two opposing camps, it leaves some of us very uncomfortable. For example, I find that the dialoguers often explain their approach in ways that leave me no choice but to stay out of their camp. Theologians representing the dialog cause often do sound relativistic; some of them even insist that interreligious dialog is an important phase in our "evolution" toward a new "global theology" to which various religions will contribute their particular "hypotheses" about ultimate reality.

I cannot accept a call to interreligious dialog that rejects Christianity's claims to uniqueness. And, frankly, I know Jews and Muslims who would also reject that approach. They do not want their claims to theological uniqueness reduced to mere "hypotheses" about spiritual things. There are genuine disagreements between the different religions. In the final analysis, the choice between religious perspectives has to do with mutually exclusive truth-claims about reality and goodness. No amount of dialog will make these differences go away.

But this does not mean that I'm a consistently comfortable resident of the evangelizing camp. My fellow evangelizers do sometimes (and I stress the *sometimes)* tend toward dogmatism and imperialism—especially in reaction to the relativistic statements of many dialoguers. But that does not mean they're right in rejecting dialog altogether.

I want an evangelizing Christianity that is open to civil dialog with non-Christians. So I look for ways of transcending these polarized positions. There is much to be gained from holding firmly to Christian truth-claims while genuinely engaging other people in serious discussion.

Transcending the Polarization

I work closely with Jewish organizations on projects having to do with religious liberty and other issues of public concern. A newspaper reporter once asked how I, an evangelical, could have such a close association with Judaism: "Don't you evangelicals try to evangelize Jews?"

I said that I do believe it's important to share my faith in Jesus Christ with non-Christians, including Jewish people. But I also think it's wrong, I told him, to treat Jews as nothing more than evangelistic prospects.

He quoted my comment in his news story, and when it was published both Jews and Christians asked me to explain these remarks further. Understandably, each group focused on a different aspect of what I had said. I was glad for the chance to elaborate on the subject, since it is an important one.

I believe in evangelism. I want to talk about my faith in Jesus Christ with my Jewish friends, and I support ongoing efforts to communicate the gospel. I would be unfaithful to my evangelical convictions if I ignored the clear biblical call to present the evangel—the good news that Jesus is the heaven-sent Son of God—to all people, including Jewish people.

But I also feel a strong need to *listen* to Jews. Even if I thought they were unwilling to listen to my views (which has not been my usual experience), I would still find conversation with them worthwhile. Jewish people have much to teach me about Judaism and about their perspectives on the teachings and actions of the Christian community. They are also helpful allies in many aspects of the struggle for public righteousness. And parallel benefits can be gained from promoting better understanding of and cooperation with Muslims, Hindus, Mormons and other religious communities.

The Value of Complementarity

It is important, I think, to value both evangelism and dialog without reducing the one to the other. The two activities have a complementary relationship.

Indeed, dialog can be an important strategy for evangelism— a fact that's been recognized by evangelicals who call for "relational evangelism." In many situations, the best way to evangelize people is to establish strong bonding relationships with them: listening to them, identifying with their hopes and fears, gaining their trust. Then, when we do have the chance to talk with them about the gospel, they can accept our words as an expression of *love for them*. The empathic give-and-take of this approach is essentially dialogic in nature.

That is good and noble. But it's important that all dialog with persons of other religious groups not be *merely* a strategy for evangelism. We mustn't set these relationships up in such a way that our efforts will be a failure if the relationships don't develop into evangelistic opportunities.

A case in point: There are different strands of Islamic thought and practice. Not every Muslim is an ardent supporter of the views of the prominent religious and political leaders in the Islamic world. Yet when Arab countries are at odds with American interests, Muslim citizens in the United States often come under cruel harassment—regardless of their political views.

I have attended interreligious gatherings in Southern California where this problem has been discussed. Local Muslim leaders have explained their own point of view and have begged the leaders of other religious communities to speak out against the harassment of American Muslims. The response has been positive. Jews, Christians, Hindus, Buddhists and others have together asked their constituencies to oppose the mistreatment of their Muslim neighbors.

This kind of dialog aims directly at better understanding and cooperation on important issues. Such efforts have little direct connection to evangelism—but they are very worthwhile. One need not be a "relativistic dialoguer" to want Muslim children to be free from harassment as they walk to school. Christians ought to care about these things, quite apart from questions about evangelistic opportunities. Whether the persecuted people are Buddhists in Vietnam or the Bahai sect in Iran or Jews in Poland or Baptists in Cuba, we need to speak out against injustice and oppression. And interreligious dialog can often help us gain the appropriate information and sensitivities.

Talking About Religion Proper

Now we should consider some important questions. Except for evangelistic purposes, is it really worth our while to attempt dialog about God and human nature and salvation? How can a true Christian have genuine "dialog" with a Muslim on spiritual topics? Doesn't a commitment to dialog mean that I'm willing to follow the conversation wherever it leads, even if it means changing my basic convictions? How could I ever agree to *that* kind of process?

These are not cranky questions. They express important concerns. I have to admit it: if entering into dialog with Muslims means that I must be willing to set aside my belief in the uniquely redemptive work of Christ, then I cannot do it. For me that is one of several nonnegotiable convictions.

What, then, *can* dialog teach us about spiritual matters?

"All truth is God's truth" is a venerable affirmation of the Christian tradition. And the mainstream of that tradition has never meant by this that spiritual truth is limited to what is explicitly taught in the Bible. As God's Word, the Bible is a direct *source* of truth. But it also helps us *test* claims to truth that come to us from other sources. Consider how the French mystic Simone Weil described the Christian's search for truth: "Christ likes us to prefer truth to him because, before being Christ, he is truth. If one turns aside from him to go toward the truth, one will not go far before falling into his arms."[1]

I find this comment intriguing. I also have to admit that Weil's way of putting the point makes me a little nervous. I balk at her suggestion that Christ wants us to value truth more than we value him. But I also know that Simone Weil never meant to suggest that we should not be totally committed to Christ. Her writings are rich expressions of deep devotion to her Lord.

What Weil is pointing to, I think, is the need to have such a total trust in Christ that we are not afraid to follow the truth wherever it leads us. He is "the true light, which enlightens everyone" (Jn 1:9). Jesus is *the* Truth. We do not have to be afraid, then, to enter into dialog with people from other religious traditions. If we find truth in what they say, we must step out in faith to reach for it—Jesus' arms will be there to catch us!

Interreligious dialog, then, can be an activity that we Christians undertake *in Christ.* The apostle Paul proclaims an important truth when he tells the Colossians that in Christ "all things hold together" (Col 1:17). The Son of God also holds the "all things" of other religions together. His Spirit is everywhere at work. No religious conversation can address matters that take place outside of his sovereign rule.

I cannot put my faith in Christ as Savior on the negotiating table in my discussions with other religionists. But I can come to the conversation with a genuine openness to learning new things about the scope of Christ's "hidden" authority and power. And these lessons can in turn reveal to us new things about others and about ourselves. Mark Heim makes this point well:

> [T]he better we know [other] faiths from the inside, the better we will sense where in a deep sense we can affirm them and where in our dialogue we must speak critically, as we are willing to listen. We must be very sensitive to their understandings of us, for they will teach us where we, within the supposed security of *the* way and truth and life, are in fact moving away from the very God we confess and proclaim.[2]

Asking Questions

I once heard an African Christian leader tell what it had been like for him to turn away from animistic religion to embrace Christ. "There were many things in my tribe's religious stories that *prepared* me for the gospel. When I first heard the story of Jesus, it did not strike me as a completely new and strange thing. What I said to myself was, 'Aha! So *that* is the answer!' "

This man first experienced Christ as the answer to questions that he had long been asking from within the framework of another religion. This should not surprise us. St. Augustine's oft-quoted prayer expresses a profound fact about the human condition: our hearts are restless until they rest in God. The spiritual restlessness that characterizes the human quest can find fulfillment only in Christ. Interreligious dialog can be an important way for us to understand better the ways in which our human restlessness is expressed in different religious settings.

Bishop Stephen Neill was a great missionary-theologian who spent many decades in India. He passionately pursued interreligious dialog, but always out of a deep conviction that Jesus is the only true Savior of humankind. His comments about Hindu-Christian relationships highlight the importance of interreligious conversations in which we probe together the questions, and the answers, that shape our lives:

[T]he Christian task is to live out the life of Jesus Christ before the eyes of [others]. They cannot see him. They will not see him, unless they can see him in the lives of his followers. If Christians are as different from others as they ought to be, questions may arise in the minds of those who watch them. This may give the Christian the opportunity to sharpen up these questions in the enquiring mind, to suggest that perhaps the answers to such questions as are given in the Hindu system are not entirely satisfactory, and lovingly point those who are willing to listen to the one in whom all human questions can receive their all-sufficient answer, the Lord Jesus Christ.[3]

9
Christian Leadership in a Pluralistic World

• • •

"THE FILM INDUSTRY is an insane asylum—and the lunatics are in charge!"

For a moment I thought I'd been transported back to the days of my youth, when I regularly heard fundamentalist preachers condemn the evils of the film industry. But the man who was speaking was no backwoods revivalist. He held an important job in Hollywood. Lately, however, he had begun to wonder whether he could maintain Christian integrity in his chosen career.

He is not alone in his struggles. A young journalist friend regularly worries that she is violating her Christian standards in satisfying her employers' understanding of what "the news" is all about. Another friend, a lawyer, has a hard time seeing how he can serve Christ in his field of corporate law. A state legislator is not sure that he can continue to be a politician without losing his soul.

Each of these Christians is struggling with the challenge of convicted civility. They are recognized as leaders in their secular settings—but they are not sure they *want* to have this recognition. Can a Christian really lead with integrity in an environment where her values and beliefs seem to be regularly compromised?

I have no simple answer to this important question. But I do have a bias on the subject. I am inclined to tell such people that they ought to hang in there and keep trying to exercise leadership. There really are no thoroughly "secular" areas of life. "The earth is the LORD's and all that is in it" (Ps 24:1)—and this includes Hollywood and the navy and Harvard and the Minnesota legislature.

But I also know that obeying the gospel sometimes requires that we separate ourselves from degrading institutions and activities. Some institutions and activities on the Lord's earth these days cannot be led in a Christian manner.

Still, let's be slow to concede defeat. I want Christians to provide leadership in diverse spheres of human interaction. In order to think about how we might do this, we need to start with some comments about leadership in general.

Transforming Leadership

James MacGregor Burns is a master of the history and theory of leadership. In his detailed scholarly study of the topic, entitled *Leadership,* Burns not only describes the ways in which great leaders have gone about their tasks but also gives a helpful account of the way leaders *ought* to lead.

The most common pattern of leadership is what Burns calls *transactional*. This is what is going on when the relationship between a leader and followers is based on some sort of trade-off. Both sides want something out of the arrangement: an interest group wants a politician to promote its cause, and the politician wants the support of that interest group in the next election. With this "transaction" in mind, the group accepts the politician's leadership.

Burns is realistic enough to know that transactional leadership cannot be completely eradicated. Nor is it necessarily an evil kind of leadership, if it is kept within proper bounds. But it can also degenerate into what Burns calls a "Machiavellian" arrangement. And that *is* bad, says Burns, because the Machiavellian leader is not really a leader at all. In the Machiavellian arrangement, the real goal is to "manage and manipulate other persons rather than to *lead* them."[1]

The best leadership is what Burns labels the *transforming* kind. This happens when both leaders and followers are willing to be changed by their relationship—each party wants to be raised "to higher levels of motivation and morality," so that their interaction will have "a transforming effect on both."[2]

Burns's distinctions are very important for civil Christians who want to exercise leadership in the world beyond the church.

Receptivity
Transforming leaders are receptive to others. We cannot hope to bring about effective change unless we are willing to *be* changed. This is a profoundly biblical idea. But it also a risky one to pursue.

I have a hunch about what is going on with some Christians who worry about being "compromised" by their involvement in non-Christian settings. I suspect they are being influenced in some *good* ways by their work, but they're nervous about how to interpret this experience.

This is what happened to a missionary I once met. He and his family had spent several years in a Third World village, and now they were home on furlough. "I have a very different attitude toward that village now from when I first got there," he reported. "I went there filled with all kinds of things I wanted to teach the people there. And I still have a strong desire to make the gospel come alive in that place. But I also feel that our family has learned much more than we have taught!"

Many Christians in the corporate and public "mission fields" of North America have a similar experience. They want to make the gospel come alive in their work. They entered their chosen arena—politics, entertainment, academia, business—aware that they would encounter much that they'd find distasteful. And this does happen. But they're also finding out that things are not always cut and dried. They realize that people working in this field must contend with many complexities and nuances.

They begin to feel the burden of all this. They find that they're learning as much as they're teaching. And they worry that perhaps they've bought into worldly values, that their Christian sensitivities are being dulled.

Of course, it may be that their sensitivities *are* being dulled. This is what makes it all so risky. But it may also be that some Christian sensitivities are being *expanded*. As transforming leaders, we will want to see our interactions with others as opportunities for expansion.

Civility means a willingness to be changed by our efforts at leadership. When we enter the place God has called us to serve, we should not expect to stay the same. Nor should we *want* to. Two important kinds of leaders in the Old Testament were the prophet and the priest. These two types have often been used by theologians to illustrate two different mediating roles in Hebrew society. The prophet mediated God's will to the people; the prophetic message typically begins with "Thus says the Lord." The priest, on the other hand, mediated the people's concerns to God; representing the people, the priest brought their confessions of sin and their deepest concerns before God.

Convicted Christians have often entered the public square as prophets. We want to tell people what God expects of them. And that is a legitimate role. God does expect us to represent the divine concern for righteousness and justice in public life.

But the priestly role is also crucial. Indeed, it is usually a necessary preparation for exercising the prophetic role. Until people have been sure that we have heard and understood their concerns, they probably will not listen to our prophetic messages. Transforming leadership requires that we genuinely listen to others, that we be empathically open to their point of view on matters that concern them deeply. Only by approaching them as priests can we hope to relate to them as prophets.

But this priestly identification with others is not merely "strategic"—as if we could go through the motions of listening to non-Christians for a while in order to gain a hearing for our message. Genuine listening involves a willingness to be changed by what we hear. We cannot hope to transform others without a commitment to being transformed ourselves.

In Jesus we see how the priestly and prophetic functions can be combined. Jesus is the Word from God, but he is also the Servant who takes our fears and temptations upon himself.

Jesus is the supreme example of a transforming leader who is deeply affected by the people he wants to lead.

This is clearly shown in the shortest verse in the Bible—John 11:35, which the King James Version renders in the stark sentence "Jesus wept." At this moment Jesus is about to raise Lazarus from the dead. But he does not merely walk into a tragic situation and demonstrate his power. He is deeply moved by the grief of Lazarus' family and friends, and he pauses to allow that sorrow to fill his own soul.

There are boundaries around Christians' openness to being changed by others. Our willingness to be changed by our encounters with other people cannot be a completely open-ended, "anything-goes" commitment. Christians are not called to be chameleons.

The apostle Paul is clear about this issue. In 1 Corinthians 9 he describes how he relates to different groups in different ways. "I have become all things to all people," he says. But this does not mean that he is unprincipled, for he immediately goes on to confess: "I do it all for the sake of the gospel" (1 Cor 9:22-23).

Jesus' way of associating with rather unsavory people, which we mentioned briefly in an earlier chapter, is relevant here. Jesus' critics constantly griped about the Lord's willingness to sit at meals with collaborators, harlots, drunkards and the like. "Why do you eat and drink with tax collectors and sinners?" they asked him. His response made it clear that he did not condone the values of his meal partners: "I have come to call not the righteous but sinners to repentance" (Lk 5:30, 32).

Our priestly efforts in the public square must also be "for the sake of the gospel." We must never forget the divine standards that require human beings to repent of their sins. And this means that it is crucial that we know who we are and what we believe as we attempt to exercise leadership.

Finding a Middle Range

In our attempts to provide public leadership, we are not merely trying to *be changed*—we are also trying to *change* what goes on in the public arena. What about this more active side of transforming leadership? What attitudes and strategies are appropriate to this dimension of our leadership task?

People sometimes get trapped in a false choice here. They think that either we must compel people, by laws and policies, to conform to our vision *or* we have to keep our "private" convictions to ourselves. George Will addresses this question nicely when he argues that "compulsion and indifference" are not our only alternatives in the public square. Between these two alternatives, he says, lies a "broad area of persuasion, incentives and other non-coercive encouragements to better living."[3]

Will is thinking primarily of political life, and, obviously, he does not mean that compulsion and indifference are always improper political strategies. We need a public order that compels us to do some things and not to do others. And it is also appropriate for the government to be "indifferent" about a large number of beliefs and behaviors. Will's important point, however, is that not everything falls into these two categories. There are some matters about which a public order must be neither compulsive *nor* indifferent.

This point applies to other areas besides politics. For example, sometimes Christians in Hollywood will have to try to change the policies and regulations of the film industry. On the other hand, sometimes they should remain indifferent to matters about which they have strong personal convictions. But here too there is a broad range of middle ground, where a leader can work at "persuasion, incentives and other non-coercive encouragements to better living."

James MacGregor Burns also has this broad middle range in mind when he talks about patterns of transforming leadership. We can work at transforming life in a variety of ways, he tells us: "elevating, mobilizing, inspiring, exalting, uplifting, preaching, exhorting, evangelizing." To be sure, Burns observes, these endeavors can sometimes be quite "moralistic"; but such activity can bring about positive change when "it raises the level of human conduct and ethical aspiration of both leader and led, and thus it has a transforming effect on both."[4]

For Burns, transforming leadership ultimately functions as a form of *teaching*. Leading and educating, he says, go hand in hand. Transforming leaders try neither to indoctrinate nor to coerce; instead, they try to educate. Christian leaders in various spheres of activity can function as teachers, using words and deeds to introduce alternative convictions and values in their workplaces.

Good teachers really do want to have an impact on their students. But they also know that teaching can never rely primarily on coercion—and we can certainly never teach with a spirit of indifference.

Effective teachers need to be good learners. Teaching is never merely doling out information. When I stand in front of a class, I ought to want my subject matter to enrich and empower *these* students who are sitting in front of me. That means that no matter how many times I have covered the material, each classroom encounter is a new experience for me. I must attempt to engage this new group of students in such a way that I too am willing to be changed by what happens between us.

Public Teaching as Interpretation

How do we go about our teaching task as Christians who are trying to provide leadership in the larger world in which we live and work? Our public teaching ministry has many facets, but Max DePree gets to the heart of things with this succinct formulation: "The first responsibility of a leader is to define reality."[5] Leaders need to have a good picture of what is really going on around them. And they need to help others take an honest look at this reality.

How can we accomplish this? How do we help other people "define reality"?

By our "pointing" actions. We must not underestimate the power of nonverbal behavior for helping people to interpret reality.

Many of my friends who belong to Roman Catholic religious orders are happy that they are no longer required to wear traditional religious garb. I respect their feelings on this subject—I have no desire to see Catholicism return to the rules and regulations of the pre-Vatican II era.

But I must confess that I'm happy there are some Catholic "religious" who still maintain distinctive modes of dress. On a plane trip recently I sat across the aisle from a young nun. She could not have been out of her twenties, and she was dressed in completely traditional garb. A very attractive young woman, she projected calmness and serenity, and for most of the trip she seemed thoroughly engrossed in a book about spirituality.

I wish I had heeded my impulse to say something to her as we left the plane. I wanted simply to say, "Thank you for being what you are." Without saying a word, in the midst of that company of passengers, she had pointed to the reality of the kingdom of God. A person had only to look at her to be reminded that the values of Christian discipleship are still alive and well.

I feel the same way about prayer in restaurants. When I am about to eat in a public place, I often bow my head to thank God for the food. A Christian friend once challenged my reasons for doing this. "I can't imagine that you are able to manufacture genuine feelings of piety while sitting there surrounded by all of those people," he said. "I just don't do that sort of thing anymore. It always strikes me as nothing more than showing off one's spirituality in public!"

Of course, he was right in insisting that we should check our motives for that kind of public act. But it doesn't trouble me that I don't often feel very "pious" when I pray in restaurants. Nor am I offended by the suggestion that it is a kind of public "showing off." In a sense, that is precisely what it *is*.

In our increasingly secularized culture, the idea of officially sponsored spirituality in public places has come under sustained attack. Public school boards have outlawed classroom prayers. Religious symbols and songs—crosses, mangers, menorahs, Christmas carols—have been banished from the public square.

There's something to be said for this trend. I can see how some of my fellow citizens are genuinely offended by these religious displays, and I want to respect their sensitivities. But I also want them to know that I cannot simply relegate my religious convictions to the "private" sphere.

I have a right to pray in restaurants, even in a highly secularized society. It is my noncoercive way of showing others that my faith is still very much a *public* matter, in spite of the accommodations I'm willing to make for the sake of persons who are offended by organized religion. To pray in a restaurant is to interpret reality. It is to give witness to my deep conviction that when I have entered into that very public place, I am still in the presence of God. It is his restaurant. It is his food. I am his creature. These are things I want to "say" in a silent and noncoercive way, even if I don't happen to be feeling very "spiritual" at the moment.

By being willing and able to state reasons for doing and saying what we do. Shortly after presidential candidate Jimmy Carter gave his acceptance speech at the Democratic convention, he taught a Sunday-school class at his home church. A reporter was there to write a story about what he said to the class.

In class, Carter went through his speech point by point. In the speech he had expressed a concern for the poor—the reason for this, Carter explained to the class, is that the Bible says God is concerned for the oppressed and the outcast. Carter had also emphasized the importance of peacemaking—for Jesus tells us that we must be peacemakers, he explained.

Carter's acceptance speech had not been overtly "Christian." But he was willing to explain to anyone how the views he had expressed were actually grounded in his faith commitment. This seems to me an excellent example of public pedagogy.

We Christians need to remember that "official" events in the public square require a special kind of discourse. A person who uses a public platform to barrage people with explicitly Christian views will soon lose the right to be heard.

Carter knew this. But he also knew that he needed to be clear in his own mind about his Christian reasons for what he said and did. And he had to be willing to accept opportunities to speak about these things, when asked to do so, and when the setting was appropriate. He could not *make* anyone in the larger society listen to what he had to say to his Sunday-school class. But he could make his message available to others, should they choose to hear what he had to say.

This is one way in which we can heed the apostle's advice: "Always be ready to make your defense to anyone who demands from you an accounting for the hope that is in you" (1 Pet 3:15).

By appealing to agreed-upon standards. Christian disciples are committed to promoting justice, righteousness and peace. These concerns have not been banned from the public square. In the United States and other democratic countries, the traditions of public discourse have been profoundly shaped by biblical thought. To be sure, other influences have also been at work—Enlightenment rationalism and deism, for example. But even those non-Christian systems of thought echo certain biblical themes.

Just before one of the national elections in the 1970s, a magazine asked me to contribute to a forum in which various political observers would describe what they hoped the next president would be like. The only stipulation was that the contributors not mention any specific candidates. I wrote my piece, and it was published. Shortly thereafter, a friend who had read my piece sent me this wry comment: "I see that you are backing Abraham Lincoln in the coming election!"

His interpretation wasn't all that outlandish. Lincoln is my favorite presidential leader. I am especially fond of his speeches, for they make brilliant use of biblical motifs: peace, righteousness, truth, justice, repentance, forgiveness, healing. Yet they are not overtly Christian—a Jew or a Muslim or a Mormon or a Christian Scientist or a Hindu could identify with much of what Lincoln says.

Some critics might say that this is a vague and amorphous "civil religion"—but I think that would be unfair. Lincoln was speaking out of a God-centered view of reality, without insisting that his hearers accept the details of biblical faith. Lincoln's speeches would probably not be greeted with widespread enthusiasm if they were delivered today. But he is still a good model for civil Christians.

To speak about justice, truth, repentance and the like is not out of place in the public square. By making sure that such topics have high priority on the public agenda, we are insisting that these standards are an important part of the *reality* that permeates the public square. Indeed, a society that ignores such standards will not survive very long. To recognize this is to be "realistic"—to have an appropriate understanding of reality. Promoting that kind of realism is an important part of being a Christian leader.

Leading in the Asylum

What does all of this mean for my Hollywood friend who feels as if he is working among lunatics in an asylum?

I hope he'll continue working at convicted civility in the film industry. I hope he won't think that his only choices are (1) coercing others into obeying his convictions and (2) adopting an attitude of indifference. I want him to be a teacher, a transforming leader who helps to define reality for his coworkers. He can perform this teaching ministry by "pointing actions," signaling to other people that he lives in a world that is not ultimately defined by lust and greed, because it is *God's* world. He can welcome any opportunities to articulate the biblical view of reality. He can try to persuade others to join him in healthy ventures by appealing to values and convictions that are deeply embedded in their own souls. And in all of this he can demonstrate, by means of his openness to others, that true leaders know they cannot teach without learning.

Jesus himself is our supreme model for this kind of leadership.

10
When There Is No "On the Other Hand"

The Limits of Civility

• • •

TEVYE, THE JEWISH dairy farmer in the musical *Fiddler on the Roof,* lives with his wife and five daughters in czarist Russia. Change is taking place all around him, and the new patterns are nowhere more obvious to Tevye than in the relationship between the sexes. First, one of his daughters announces that she and a young tailor have pledged themselves to each other, even though Tevye has already promised her to the village butcher, a widower. Initially Tevye will not hear of his daughter's plans, but he finally has an argument with himself and decides to give in to the young lovers' wishes.

A second daughter also chooses the man she wants to marry:

an idealistic revolutionary. Tevye is rather fond of him, and, after another argument with himself, he again concedes to the changing times.

A while later, Tevye's third daughter wishes to marry. She has fallen in love with a young Gentile. This violates Tevye's deepest religious convictions: it is unthinkable that one of his daughters would marry outside the faith. Once again, he has an argument with himself. He knows that his daughter is deeply in love, and he does not want her to be unhappy. Still, he cannot deny his convictions.

"How can I turn my back on my faith, my people?" he asks himself. "If I try and bend that far, I'll break!" Tevye pauses and begins a response: "On the other hand. . . ." He pauses again, and then he shouts: "No! There *is* no other hand!"

Every person who strives for convicted civility must think about the kind of moment at which Tevye has arrived. There may well come times in our lives when civility is not enough, when we have considered all our options and find that we have come up against the limits of our convictions. To bend any further is to break.

I regularly lecture in team-taught courses on leadership. I receive more than I give in such settings. It's interesting to discuss case studies with the students, many of whom are administrators in large congregations, agencies and schools. We place a strong emphasis on listening skills, conflict management and shared decision-making. I believe strongly in all these practices. But I also insist that we talk about a time that might well come when such things are not enough to sustain us our work—when, even though all the right skills and methods and sensitivities have been used, the results cannot be squared with the claims of conscience. In such a situation we may have no other choice but to say: "No! There *is* no other hand!"

Organizational Ethics

A friend of mine thinks he is getting close to the breaking point
in his relationship with his denomination. He does not agree
with his church's official position on an issue that is important
to him. He has worked hard to change things through the
proper channels, but to no avail. In fact, it seems to him that
things have gotten worse over the past decade.

"Are there any good books on ecclesiastical ethics?" he asked
me. "I know a lot has been written about civil disobedience in
relationship to governments, but has anyone worked on what
you do when you're having a hard time living with your
church's rules and regulations?"

"Not much," I told him. "Maybe the Catholics have some stuff
on the subject in their 'canon law' literature. But I doubt that
it will be helpful to you. Someone needs to work on that!"

Someone *does* need to work on it. We need help in deciding
how to handle those situations in our churches where we are
pushed to limits of civility. And not just in our churches—also
in corporate boardrooms and families and political caucuses and
parent-teacher associations.

Whether modern times are more wicked than previous ages
is not a matter we have to decide here. But there can be no
doubt that we are surrounded by much evil. Sometimes movements and individuals come along—in society in general or in
our more limited circles—that push us beyond the bounds of
toleration. It is not difficult to think of examples: neo-Nazis, the
Ku Klux Klan, Satanists, people who want to teach our children to "be comfortable with" what we consider sexually perverse, heresy hunters in our churches—and heretics who make

it easy for the heresy hunters to pursue their work.

No simple-minded solutions are adequate. Better education, more effective communication, improved decision-making systems, new methods of conflict management—none of these will provide solutions when the disagreements run deep.

Many convicted people have found, like Tevye, that times come when there is no "on the other hand": Frederick Douglass, who fled from his master to lead the fight against slavery. Corrie ten Boom, who offered a hiding place to the oppressed. Rosa Parks, who decided while boarding the bus one afternoon in Montgomery, Alabama, that she would no longer cooperate with racial segregation. Aleksandr Solzhenitsyn, who held his moral ground against tyrants. The Chinese students in Tiananmen Square who lost their lives as they demonstrated for democracy.

We too must be ready and willing to say no when the occasion arises. We need help in understanding how to act when civility is not enough.

Borrowing from "Just War"

The just-war doctrine is meant to provide a moral framework for thinking about the legitimate use of military force. While the principles associated with just-war thinking are not derived directly from the Bible, they have been worked out over the centuries by Christian ethicists who have reflected upon the practical moral questions that arise when nations go to war.

I subscribe to this theory—and I believe just-war principles are often relevant to nonmilitary situations. As I suggested in an earlier chapter, I am especially interested in how the just-war perspective can help us to avoid a crusading spirit in our moral and spiritual warfare. Just-war teaching is meant to help us guard against an anything-goes attitude toward military campaigns; we need the same kinds of safeguards in our other "battles."

There will come times when civility alone is not adequate for dealing with our differences. But this does not mean that we can simply shift from civility to a crusading mode. We must follow moral and spiritual guidelines in all our "warfare."

What might those guidelines look like? In responding to this question I am not going to mechanically list the just-war principles, but I will be looking to them for my inspiration.

Is my cause a just one? This is a crucial place to start. We are sinners; we know it's easy to get caught up in arguments that really have little to do with questions of justice. And even if the issue is an important one, it is not inconceivable that we are arguing for the wrong position. Since several times I've changed my own mind on topics about which I felt strongly, I've learned to proceed with caution before launching a crusade.

Before we get far into a passionate controversy, then, it is important to review our case to be sure that we are on the right side of the argument. "Search me, O God, and know my heart; test me and know my thoughts" (Ps 139:23).

Am I sustained in my commitments by the wisdom of competent authorities? The appeal to the verdict of competent authorities is an important component of just-war doctrine. Indeed, over the centuries the Christian community has recognized how important it is to maintain structures of authority.

We must also honor authority in matters of spiritual warfare. That doesn't mean we can do nothing without "official" backing—in fact, at times we'll find it necessary to take a stand *against* "officialdom."

But this is no excuse to act like anarchists. To be sure, to be a Christian is to honor *divine* authority, so that no genuinely Christian act of protest will be anti-authority as such. But it is not enough to claim God's backing. God himself makes it clear in the Bible that we must respect the patterns of human authority. This means, I think, that we have to be very careful to avoid "Lone Ranger" approaches to dissent. We must seek out *communal discernment.*

But what about Martin Luther? Didn't he stand alone against the whole system of ecclesiastical (and political) authority? "Here I stand, I can do no other, God helping me." And don't we present-day Christians—including many Catholics—rightly celebrate his courageous venture?

Luther's example is indeed instructive. I have deep admiration for the great Reformer. But "here *I* stand" declarations trouble me, even when they come from the likes of Luther. Not that what he said or did was wrong. But it was dangerous. Too many Christians who came after him repeated his words and deeds without the sensitivities that marked his own deliberations.

Luther did not simply set forth his own private interpretation of things as over against the authority of the whole church. He studied both the Scriptures and the Christian tradition with great care. He also solicited the advice of trusted friends and colleagues. In these ways Luther sought out the wise counsel of the larger Christian body. He knew that we ought not to say, "There *is* no 'on the other hand' " without careful and prayerful heed to a community of discernment.

Are my motives proper? We must be careful not to pursue good causes out of bad motives. A pastor in a mainline denomination told me about a national assembly she had attended:

"We had a big fight, and I was completely on the side of the conservatives—I had no choice, since I felt the authority of the Bible was at stake. But I have to admit that I was still uneasy deep down in my soul. Sometimes I wonder what our conservative movement is actually trying to accomplish. I sometimes wonder whether we are really as committed to the goals of Christ's kingdom as we say we are!"

We need to pay careful attention to what we are actually trying to accomplish in our moral and spiritual struggles. Our cause may be utterly defensible—but is it what *really* motivates us? Have we latched onto this issue for other reasons? Were we looking for a cause that would unite our forces? Are we seeking power or revenge or publicity?

Is my move beyond mere civility a choice of last resort? This question highlights the importance of *thoroughness* in choosing strategies. In the military context, the last-resort criterion points to the need to explore all other means of conflict resolution before we opt for violent solutions. There is a parallel consideration in moral and spiritual warfare: Have we really exhausted all the resources of civility?

Civility is a commitment to keep the conversation going. It requires that we not give in easily to the temptation to cut off our efforts at empathy. We need to be sure that we haven't given up prematurely on a person or group. To use the language of negotiating strategy: we must continually ask whether there is some "win-win" outcome that we haven't yet considered.

Sometimes civil dialog is not enough; sometimes we must go beyond mere civility. Still, the basic requirements of civility are never really canceled. Christians never have a right to become *less* than civil people—our only option is to move beyond *mere* civility.

Is success likely? In a 1983 pastoral letter on peacemaking, the American Catholic bishops made a helpful comment on the just-war version of this criterion. It is important, they said, to avoid both "irrational use of force" and "hopeless resistance." But then they hastened to observe that sometimes the "defense of key values, even against great odds," is itself the kind of "success" we are aiming for.[1]

The point is not to let everything hang on pragmatic considerations. The bishops rightly warn us against this pattern of thinking—there are times when we must do what is right, regardless of the predictable results. But we must also be sure that we have really gotten to the point where positive results no longer matter.

I know someone who quit an important position in an organization as a protest against a decision made by others. Years later, a lonely and bitter man, he wondered aloud whether he had acted too hastily. In some circumstances, what we think at the time to be a bold moral stand may prove a futile gesture that will be quickly forgotten by everyone but ourselves.

Are the means I am employing proportionate to the good goals I want to promote? We must not avoid cost-benefit analysis. "Trade-off" issues are important. If I cut off the civil conversation at this point, what will be the effects? Do I really want them? Are they worth it, given all the other things I care about?

Some Christian scholars have argued that Martin Luther's decision to break with the Church of Rome actually failed to satisfy this proportionality criterion. Considered by itself, they say, his actions make good sense. But look at the effect his decision has had on overall patterns of churchly life: he inspired a spirit of divisiveness. Luther's "Here I stand" was repeated too many times; leaders with less noble causes followed his example by rebelling against legitimate authority.

I am not prepared to concur in this analysis, but the questions these critics raise are legitimate. God wants us to take responsibility for our actions. This means that we must reflect carefully on the possible outcomes of what we are thinking about doing.

Kindness in Warfare

St. Augustine was one of the first Christian thinkers to spell out some of the basic just-war principles. His primary intent was not to oppose pacifism, but to counter the religious devotion to violence that pervaded the pagan world. People in his day were dedicated to the service of the gods of war. Military pursuits were invested with a spiritual value.

Augustine believed that violence was sometimes morally necessary in a sinful world. But he also knew that warfare was a dangerous business from a Christian point of view. There is a real threat, he once wrote to a friend, that in punishing evildoers we will succeed in conquering our external enemies, only to be destroyed by "the enemy within"—our own "depraved and distorted hearts." This is why, he went on, we have to develop "those kindly feelings which keep us from returning evil for evil." If we can do that, he argues, "even war will not be waged without kindness."[2]

The idea that warfare can be carried on with *kindness* may seem bizarre. But it really isn't. Treating prisoners humanely, respecting the rights of civilian populations, refusing to demand "total defeat" or "unconditional surrender" before peace negotiations can begin—these are examples of kindness in the conduct of warfare.

Augustine was insisting that Christians are never excused

from showing others the gentleness and reverence that is their due as creatures of God. And if that is true in military campaigns, it certainly applies to moral and spiritual warfare.

Civility is not enough in some situations. But I must repeat: its basic requirements are never canceled. Christians never have a right simply to cast aside kindness and gentleness. We are never justified in engaging in a no-holds-barred crusade against our opponents. Going beyond *mere* civility does not mean that we can become *less* than civil.

What does that mean, though, in real situations of conflict? What about dealing with Nazis and Satanists and people who advocate legalized incest and the heretics in our churches? What does it mean to treat *such* persons with gentleness and reverence?

It means, for one thing, that we never forget that they are indeed *persons* who are created in God's image and who are still within the reach of divine mercy. It means we can think about cutting off conversation with them only when it becomes clear that they are, by their clear intent to harm the lives of other persons, *asking* us to do so. And it means that we may never let go of the hope that they may yet flourish as creatures who have the potential to glorify their Maker.

Needless to say, these are difficult standards. We can't hope to live up to them without regular infusions of divine grace into our lives. But that should neither surprise nor discourage us. Dorothy Day, the saintly founder of the Catholic Worker movement, summarized the situation well in her life's motto: "It is all grace."

Without grace, civility cannot endure. And what else but grace could possibly sustain us in those moments when we have no choice but to move *beyond* civility?

11
Is Hell Uncivil?

•   •   •

I HAVE BEEN arguing in this book that people with strong, orthodox Christian convictions ought to be more civil. Now we need to face a tough question. If we are going to cultivate civility effectively, doesn't at least one of our traditional convictions have to be discarded? Can a kind, gentle person believe in hell?

Hell gets bad press among civil people. And it is not difficult to understand why. Isn't hell a very uncivil thing to believe in? Indeed, isn't it hard to imagine anything *more* uncivil than the belief that people whose basic convictions are different from ours will be punished for ever and ever?

That certainly seems like a very uncivil belief. Indeed, hell seems so distasteful that I'm nervous about bringing up the subject. But I have to be candid about my own conviction: I do accept the traditional teaching regarding the reality of hell. At the same time, as I hope has become clear by now, I want very much to be a civil person.

Many people would say at this point that I have set myself an impossible task: hell and civility just do not go together. That is the challenge I want to take up here.

The Traditional Teaching

When I say I *accept* the traditional teaching regarding the reality of hell, I am choosing my words carefully. "Accept" has a passive feel to it—and that is appropriate in my case. I'm not especially fond of the doctrine of hell. It is not the kind of teaching I would have thought up on my own. I don't want people to go to hell; in fact, I hope that no one actually goes there. If hell turns out to be empty, I will have absolutely no complaints.

The alternative to the belief that some people will be consigned to hell is the teaching called universalism: that everyone will be saved in the end. I find universalism to be a very pleasing doctrine. I wish it were true. But, unfortunately, I simply have not been able to convince myself that universalism is defensible. The New Testament impresses me over and over again with its very serious warnings against unbelief. Take John 3:36, for example: "Whoever believes in the Son has eternal life; whoever disobeys the Son will not see life, but must endure God's wrath." This seems to me to be fairly straightforward and decisive.

So I accept that hell is a reality, though I don't relish the truth of this teaching. A few years ago I attended the funeral of a friend's son. The young man had been heavily involved in drug trafficking and was killed in the midst of an armed robbery. He had consistently rejected his Christian mother's pleas that he straighten out his life. At his funeral service, I fervently prayed that he had not, in his death, placed himself beyond the reach of God's grace. But I have yet to reconcile my pleas with what seems the most plausible way of reading the biblical warnings against unbelief. And I want very much to be faithful to what the Bible teaches.

This does not mean that I endorse popular Christian images of eternal punishment. Neither does it mean that I interpret all the biblical imagery about hell in a literalist fashion—I don't believe, for example, that hell is literally both a lake of fire and a region of "outer darkness."

Nor do I want to be associated with the view of God that is often associated with clichéd images of eternal damnation. Much popular mythology about hell—so easily satirized in "Far Side" and "Boffo" cartoons—portrays God as a small-minded and petty deity who is especially fond of small-minded and petty people.

What I do accept is the church's traditional teaching, stripped of all the excesses of popular imagery regarding literal hellfire and divine vindictiveness. On this view, as I understand it, the God of the Bible hates the sin that disrupts his creation. He is very angry about human rebellion, and he is preparing the world for a day when his rejection of wickedness will be public and final. These themes tell us something important about the character of God: the biblical God cannot easily be squeezed into romanticized "God-is-love" packages.

One morning the coffee-break conversation at a school where

I was teaching took up the topic of hell. We all agreed about hell's reality, because we were convinced that this is what the Bible teaches. But we also admitted that it was hard to stress this teaching in our own thought and practice. Hell was not a topic we were fond of discussing.

Just a few days later I attended a conference where the worship services were led by African-American urban pastors. "Fire-and-brimstone" themes dominated their preaching. Upon reflection, I realized that these preachers spoke much more of social injustice—especially the sins committed against the poor and the oppressed—than did preachers I was accustomed to hearing. These black pastors knew firsthand what it's like for people to be denied their dignity as human beings. Racial discrimination was all too concrete for them. They lived in a world where hunger and malnutrition and desperate poverty were the norm.

Was there an important lesson in this? It may be that our failure to think and speak about divine judgment is closely related to our refusal to face the reality of human evil. Even more important: it may have something to do with how much we actually *feel* the reality of human evil.

Observers of spiritual trends tell us that fewer Christians these days believe in hell. Could there be a connection between this fact and the social blinders that many of us wear? If so— if we are downplaying God's wrath because we really can't imagine what God might be all that angry about—then maybe we need to learn some theological lessons from Christians whose lives are permeated with poverty and persecution.

Understanding Hell
One of the most sensible books on hell I have read is by Peter

Toon, a British Anglican. Toon refuses to embrace universalism, but he also insists that we must exercise great care in speaking about hell. We have no business, for example, telling others that they will go to hell. Nor do we have any biblical justification for predicting how large hell's population will be: "It may be many, a few, or none. God alone knows," Toon insists.

The Bible employs rich and diverse imagery in speaking about hell. Given its lack of systematic treatment, Toon advises, we should "refuse to go beyond the minimum detail"; we must avoid getting involved in disputes about the nature of the afterlife and offering glib defenses of the "need" for a hell.[1]

The Minimum Detail

So far I may seem to be pushing an agnostic, "I-don't-know-much" approach to the doctrine of hell: we'll acknowledge that hell is *there* as a Christian teaching—but let's pay as little attention to it as we can!

That's not quite my intention, though. Toon rightly insists that we stick to "the minimum detail" in what we say and think about hell. Still, the minimum detail is packed with important content. Some of this content is relevant to the topic of civility, and it deserves to be highlighted here.

The reality of hell underscores the seriousness of sin. A denial of hell often goes hand-in-hand with a minimizing of our sinfulness. To be sure, defenders of hell can also trivialize human wickedness. There have been times, for example, when Protestants and Catholics acted as if hell were primarily a destination for the losers in the debates between them.

Today, however, few of us defend hell out of a desire to see our favorite theological enemies get their comeuppance. We're more likely these days to err in the direction of deemphasizing the wrath of God.

Sin is a deep insult against the God who made us. This is a matter where God's honor is at stake. How God will deal with the horrible evils that have plagued his creation is not something that can be addressed in catchy slogans.

Hell reinforces the importance of human freedom. The idea of human freedom is basic to my understanding of hell. It is very important for me to think of hell as a freely chosen state of being.

In emphasizing human freedom, I've had to reject the idea that hell is God's "external" punishment on people because of their misdeeds. There is an important issue at stake in the choice between these two concepts. Is hell primarily something that God inflicts upon sinners, or is it a condition that they inflict upon themselves?

The idea that God "sends" people to hell for punishment suggests a rather passive role for people—they are *acted upon* by God in the afterlife. According to those who defend this view, hell is where God finally "gives" sinners the punishment they have coming to them. Those who criticize this view, on the other hand, are inclined to view the kind of people who would be sent to this kind of hell as *victims*. Does anyone really deserve to be punished for all eternity? they ask. Is it fair to torment someone for ever and ever for misdeeds that have occurred within a limited life span?

Both sides of this argument seem to me to be based on the false assumption that hell is a punishment imposed from outside. Instead, I think of hell as the culmination of a person's own freely chosen life-plan. Hell isn't what God does to people; it is what people do to themselves.

I am fond of the well-known formulation of the Westminster Catechism: our "chief end" as human beings is "to glorify God and to enjoy him forever." Because of our sin, however, we are incapable of mustering up the resources to live out a life-plan that glorifies God. This is why we are desperately in need of divine grace. If we do open ourselves up to God's freely offered grace, we are empowered for a life-plan that will allow us to be all God meant us to be. If we refuse that grace, we will follow a plan of living that distorts the good purposes for which we are created.

Hell is the ultimate and inevitable consequence of a persistent refusal of divine grace. It is separation from God—a state of affairs where we have finally cut ourselves off from the possibility of being healthy human creatures.

But doesn't the Bible use imagery that suggests an active *consigning* of people to hell? It surely does. Sinners will be *thrown* "into the outer darkness, where there will be weeping and gnashing of teeth" (Mt 8:12), and the wicked will be "*thrown* into the lake of fire" (Rev 20:15).

But it's important to recognize that this is indeed *imagery*. We would be misled if we took the "throwing" imagery literally, just as we would if we insisted that hell is both a literal outer darkness and a literal lake of fire. All these images are meant to point to the horrors of an existence that has finally been cut off from the possibility of God's mercy. They are not meant as literal snapshots.

The picture of people being "thrown" into hell needs to be balanced by the strong biblical emphasis on our own active role in separating ourselves from God. Psalm 7 reports that God is preparing "deadly weapons" to use against the wicked (v. 13); but it immediately goes on to say that the wicked themselves are digging the hole into which they will fall when "their mischief returns upon their own heads, and on their own heads their violence descends" (vv. 15-16). Similarly, Romans 1 emphasizes how God *gives people over* to the wicked designs they have chosen. C. S. Lewis says somewhere that the door to hell is finally shut from the inside. Hell happens when God finally allows people to close themselves off completely from his divine presence. This is the final outcome for people who insist that the Serpent's lie in the Garden of Eden is a truth—that we can indeed be our own gods. The doctrine of hell teaches that God will not violate my basic choice of a life-plan; even if I insist on forever going it alone, I must be allowed to stick with my decision.

The Jesuit theologian John Sachs captures this point in just the right way:

> Because human beings are free, Christianity recognizes a godlike dignity in them. No other ideology takes human beings this seriously. In this sense, the Church's teaching about hell says: "You count. You have ultimate significance. What you do in your life is not meaningless; it has final worth."[2]

Hell means that the final settling of accounts is in the hands of God. The Christian teaching about the Last Judgment raises many questions that seem impossible to answer on the basis of the available evidence. How will God finally deal with people who have never heard the gospel but who have lived as well as they could in the light available to them? What about individuals who have pursued very wicked life-plans, only to cry out for divine mercy with their dying breath?

Sometimes questions of this sort are asked in a highly speculative manner—but not always. They can also be asked out of a very deep and personal sense of urgency.

I know a woman who was reared in a Christian home but does not herself profess to be a Christian. Indeed, she gets very angry when anyone tries to talk to her about the Gospel. I also know that this woman was very cruelly abused by her father, who was a highly regarded Christian leader. When I hear her expressions of anger toward Christianity, I hear an unspeakable hurt over the abuse that she suffered at the hands of a "saint."

For a long time this woman lived in a very rebellious manner. Lately, though, she has begun to make much healthier choices. But she still refuses to have anything to do with Christianity.

Here is my hunch. I think God understands her intense and abiding pain. I think he sees the psychological barriers that make it so difficult for her to hear as "good news" anything that she associates with her father's hypocrisy. And I think God will deal with her on the basis of what she was able to handle spiritually in her deeply wounded condition.

I also have a hunch about how God will deal with at least one very wicked person. My hunch is that Hitler is in hell. The life-plan that he deliberately and consistently pursued was so evil that I cannot imagine any other outcome for him but eternal separation from the mercy of God.

Those are my hunches about how God will deal with two people who have not professed a faith in the gospel. And to tell the truth, I hope both of my hunches are true. I want the abused woman to be saved in the end, whether or not she can bring herself to ask God to save her. And I want Hitler to be cut off from the possibility of mercy—every time I read accounts of the Holocaust I find myself desperately hoping that the perpetrators will know the fullness of the divine wrath.

But those are personal hunches, based on my wishes. They

are not exercises in sound theology, and I can't use them as excuses to avoid my responsibilities. I still need to pray, for example, that the abused woman will consciously experience the healing power of the gospel in her life. And I also need to pray that I won't be overcome by a spirit of vindictiveness against people like Hitler.

It is not spiritually beneficial for me to spend too much time nurturing the hunches I have just described. I know that there is no salvation apart from the redeeming work of Jesus Christ, that no one can be right with God without accepting the basic claims of the gospel. It is up to God, of course, to decide just when and how people have properly "accepted" his offer of salvation in Christ. I have no business deciding that some people really do not need to wrestle here and now with the gospel message. Nor is it healthy for me to spend much time thinking about how God will ultimately punish his enemies.

The final accounting is not up to us. "Thy kingdom come, thy will be done." Our obligation is to act in the light of what we *know* we are to do: "He has told you, O mortal, what is good; and what does the LORD require of you but to do justice, and to love kindness, and to walk humbly with your God?" (Mic 6:8).

Lessons for Civility

I do not talk much about hell. My sense is that convicted Christians have often done too much talking on this subject. We have regularly said more than the Bible permits us to say. To admit this error, and to try to correct it by paying attention to "the minimum detail," is not liberalism or compromise. It is an important exercise in Christian honesty.

But does this mean that Christians are to work at being civil *in spite of* the fact that they seem to be required to believe in the reality of hell? No. To put it in those terms is to fail to see how the doctrine of hell fits within the contours of Christian civility.

Human wickedness is real. God respects human freedom. And God alone will decide our final destiny in the light of what he knows about the life-plans we've chosen. These three themes are crucial to my understanding of civility.

No attempt to be civil will be biblically adequate if it downplays the reality of evil. Civility cannot mean relativism. All beliefs and values are not on a moral par. When we show kindness and reverence toward people with whom we disagree about important issues, it cannot be because we don't care about the ultimate questions of truth and goodness.

Christian civility takes human freedom seriously. I may want people to believe as I do about some basic matters—but what I want is for them to *choose* to see things that way. This means that I must rely on testimony and persuasion in presenting my views to them. Civil Christians will be very reluctant to endorse moral and religious programs that rely on coercion.

And Christian civility will display the patience that comes from knowing that the final accounting belongs to God. He alone will decide how to settle accounts with people who have consistently dishonored his loving purposes: "Beloved, never avenge yourselves, but leave room for the wrath of God; for it is written, 'Vengeance is mine, I will repay, says the Lord' " (Rom 12:19).

The Imperative

Is hell uncivil? I think not. Hell is about God's honor and our freedom. Those are very important issues. To care about such things is to care about human flourishing. But that does not

mean that civil Christians should devote much time and energy
to thinking and talking about hell itself. There are more helpful
ways of highlighting the importance of God's honor and human
freedom.

I like the emphasis of the Reformed theologian G. C. Berkouwer when he writes about the topic of hell. He observes that
when a questioner asked Jesus, "Lord, will only a few be
saved?" Jesus began his answer with a command: "Strive to
enter through the narrow door" (Lk 13:23-24). This may seem
an evasive response, says Berkouwer, but it really is not. This
is Jesus' answer to the question. We are not to understand the
hereafter by speculating about the demographics or geography
of heaven and hell. The appropriate mode of understanding is
to obey the will of God and to invite others to do so also.[3]

"Strive to enter through the narrow door." The stakes are
very high—they have eternal significance. Caring deeply about
how people respond to *this* imperative can be an important way
of being a gentle and reverent Christian.

12
Abraham Kuyper, Meet Mother Teresa

*The Problem
of Triumphalism*

• • •

IN THE PREVIOUS two chapters we've explored the boundary lines of mere civility. How do we know when we've exhausted the resources of polite dialog? In what sense, if any, is the traditional teaching about hell a stumbling block for civil Christians? These are important questions. The God of the Bible cannot be defined in terms of mere "niceness." Because of who God is, convictedness—a deep commitment to the standards of right and wrong—is woven into the very fabric of the universe.

Both revelation and experience make it clear, however, that God has chosen not to rush to judgment. The certainty that God will triumph does not give us license to act as if we had already purchased the victory over evil. Learning civility is learning to imitate God's patient dealings with his rebellious creatures. In our final two chapters, we will explore these two themes of triumph and patience.

The Reign of Jesus

Recently someone asked me what Christian thinker had most influenced my social-political thinking. I did not hesitate for a moment in coming up with the answer: Abraham Kuyper.

Not too many people in North America have ever heard of Abraham Kuyper, but he was an important figure in the Netherlands. Kuyper, who lived from 1837 to 1920, founded a Christian political party, and he even served as prime minister of the Netherlands during the early years of the twentieth century. He was also a gifted philosopher-theologian, a well-known educator, and a prolific journalist.[1]

And Abraham Kuyper was an ardent Calvinist who believed passionately in the sovereignty of God. I like his brand of Calvinism very much. Calvinists sometimes have had a reputation for not being activists. After all, the popular argument goes, if God is in control of everything, then nothing much rides on our accomplishments.

That was not the way Kuyper saw things. He insisted that God wants Christians to be active in *showing forth* the divine rule. Jesus is King, and we are his subjects. This means that we must try to be obedient to the reign of Jesus in all areas of our lives: family relationships, friendships, business, politics, leisure time, art, science, farming. In whatever we do, we must seek to glorify God.

"Mine!"

My favorite Kuyper quotation comes from a speech that he once gave before a university audience in Amsterdam. He was arguing that scholarship is an important form of Christian discipleship. Since scholarship deals with God's world, it has to be done in such a way that it honors Christ. Kuyper concluded with this ringing proclamation: "There is not one square inch of the entire creation about which Jesus Christ does not cry out, 'This is mine! This belongs to me!' "

This strong sense of Christ's cosmic lordship is thoroughly biblical: "For in him all things in heaven and on earth were created, things visible and invisible, whether thrones or dominions or rulers or powers—all things have been created through him and for him" (Col 1:16). To emphasize Jesus' universal rule in this way is very important for a healthier understanding of what we have come to think of as "the ministries of the laity." The home, the brokerage firm, the auto dealership, the gym and the concert hall—all belong to Christ. Our work in these settings is as much Christian ministry as anything that goes on in a church building.

When Kuyper pictured Jesus as crying out that everything in the universe *belongs* to him, he was not suggesting that the Lord is a self-centered property owner. Jesus isn't like a toddler who screeches "Mine!" as he yanks toys away from his playmates. Kuyper knew that for Jesus, "This is mine!" expresses a love so deep that he was willing to suffer and die in order to rescue his creation from sin.

Empire Discipleship

I discovered Kuyper's social thought at an important time in my life—as a graduate student in a secularized university environment during the turbulent 1960s. I was drawn toward political activism, but I wasn't quite sure how it could be inte-

grated with my Christian faith. It was difficult in those days
to find any good writings on the subject by my fellow evangelicals. But my evangelical propensities were strong enough that
I was not satisfied with the "radical Christian" and "social gospel" perspectives that were available to me.

Then I discovered Kuyper. His theology was thoroughly orthodox, and he had a warm evangelical faith. But he also had
a strong sense of Christ's cosmic lordship over all of creation,
and he had worked out the implications of this perspective for
his own social activism. This was just what I needed. His views
"took" in my own life and thought. They continue to influence
me in deep ways.

But for all that, I worry about a tendency that is often engendered by Kuyper's kind of perspective. It's the tendency to
follow this line of reasoning: since Christ owns all those square
inches of the creation, our mandate as Christians is to go forth
and conquer them in his name!

I can't dismiss this call as simply mistaken. In fact, I've
regularly expressed sentiments of this sort myself, and I will
probably continue to do so. To state things in such terms may
sound "imperialistic," but it's difficult to get rid of all traces of
imperialism while remaining faithful to Scripture. If the cos-
mos is indeed Christ's *empire*—and it is—then Christian discipleship will inevitably have some imperialist themes built into
it.

The problem is not so much, then, with the actual claims we
make about Christ's cosmic lordship, as with the tone with
which we make them. What bothers me specifically is the spirit
of Christian *triumphalism.* I detect this spirit sometimes when
I'm reading Kuyper. I see it also in various programs for "lib-
erating the poor and the oppressed" in the name of the gospel.

And there certainly has been more than enough triumphalism in the preachings of the New Christian Right: "The humanists have taken over the educational system. We must reclaim our schools for the cause of Christ!" "Let's get out there and show our politicians that Christ is King, and we won't have them poaching on his territory!"

Knowing About the Triumph

Let's examine the triumphalist spirit more closely. Just what is it? For me, the key word is *spirit*. I do not like triumphalism, but one can't simply characterize it as some sort of intellectual error. Triumphalists believe strongly in the triumph of Christ—and that in itself is not wrong. What makes triumphalism a worrisome thing is the spirit that energizes many programs of Christian action.

In order to see where triumphalists go wrong, we need to set forth three basic truths about Christ's triumphant ministry.

First, *Christ has indeed been victorious over sin.* We must not lose sight of this foundational truth. There really is a triumph. Not only is Christ the creator of all rulers and authorities in the universe, but he has also defeated their sinful designs by his death on the cross: "He disarmed the rulers and authorities and made a public example of them, triumphing over them in it" (Col 2:15).

The victory is cosmic in scope. Because of what Jesus has accomplished we can be sure that the powers of injustice, oppression, disease and death have been defeated. To quote again the jubilant refrain from the carol by Isaac Watts: "He comes to make his blessings flow / far as the curse is found."

Second, *Christ's followers are beneficiaries of his cosmic victory.* Theologians tell a story to illustrate how Christ's triumph presently benefits our lives: Imagine a city under siege. The enemy that surrounds the city will not let anyone or anything enter or leave. Supplies are running low, and the citizens are fearful.

But in the dark of the night, a spy sneaks through the enemy lines. He has rushed to the city to tell the people that in another place the main enemy force has been defeated; the leaders have already surrendered. The people do not need to be afraid. It is only a matter of time until the besieging troops receive the news and lay down their weapons.

Similarly, we may seem now to be surrounded by the forces of evil—disease, injustice, oppression, death. But the enemy has actually been defeated at Calvary. Things are not the way they seem to be. It is only a matter of time until it becomes clear to all that the battle is really over.

This is an apt illustration. It accounts for both the fact of Christ's victory and the all-too-obvious siege under which we live. To know about the divine triumph is to experience the confidence that is so vibrantly expressed by the apostle:

Who will separate us from the love of Christ? Will hardship, or distress, or persecution, or famine, or nakedness, or peril, or sword? . . . No, in all these things we are more than conquerors through him who loved us. For I am convinced that neither death, nor life, nor angels, nor rulers, nor things present, nor things to come, nor powers, nor height, nor depth, nor anything else in all creation, will be able to separate us from the love of God in Christ Jesus our Lord. (Rom 8:35-39)

Third, *our lives must give evidence of our confidence in Christ's victory.* It is not enough to have an inner awareness of the triumph of the cross. Our confidence must make a difference in the way we live. Here the parable of the city under siege ceases to be very helpful, since the moral of the story seems to be that we should just hold on for a little longer. If we were to push it to the limits of its usefulness, we would have to find some way in which the awareness of the good news made a significant difference in the citizens' patterns of living. The Christian life is not a mere holding action. It is active obedience. We cannot be "more than conquerors" without somehow showing it in our words and deeds.

Why Not Triumphalism?

Those are the basics on which all Christians should be able to agree. It is from this point on, however, that the triumphalist spirit can begin to take over. This happens when people think that the best way to *give evidence* of their confidence in Christ's victory is *to claim the victors' spoils.*

Right now, goodness certainly seems to be under siege in many parts of the world. Corrupt politicians hold the reins of power. Greed and lust run rampant in the marketplace. Prejudice and oppression abound.

There is no scarcity, however, of Christian triumphalist antidotes to our present predicament. One group of Christians opposes all "Band-Aid solutions" in the name of a Christian "liberation" of economic and political structures. Another movement wants to bring back all of the Old Testament civil legislation—including the death penalty for homosexuals. Other Christians are convinced that a vigorous campaign of "spiritual warfare" will exorcise the "territorial spirits" that are oppressing our towns and cities.

Back to Abraham Kuyper's "square inch" manifesto: we can see now how easily it can function as a triumphalist rallying cry. Since every square inch of the creation belongs to Christ, shouldn't we go out and conquer it all in his name? Why allow trespassers to occupy territory to which they have no rightful claim?

Again, the mistake here has to do with the spirit in which people are giving evidence of their confidence in Christ's victory. Triumphalist Christians focus on the fruits of the triumph—they want to *claim* these fruits.

What is the alternative? To realize that *claiming the spoils of Christ's victory is not the appropriate means of displaying our confidence in that victory.* When the biblical writers encourage us to show our confidence in Christ's triumph, they do not tell us to do so by claiming the victory prize here and now. Instead, we best demonstrate our participation in the benefits of Christ's redemptive work by our willingness to suffer in a Christlike manner as we await the outcome he has secured. The apostle Peter lays out this pattern of thought with simple clarity:

> Beloved, do not be surprised at the fiery ordeal that is taking place among you to test you, as though something strange were happening to you. But rejoice insofar as you are sharing Christ's sufferings, so that you may also be glad and shout for joy when his glory is revealed. (1 Pet 4:12-13)

To "be like Jesus" is not to claim the triumph and then proceed to take over what is rightly ours. It is to participate in Christ's sufferings in full confidence that our Lord has guaranteed a victorious outcome.

Christ's "Distressing Disguise"

When visitors come to Mother Teresa's community house in Calcutta to learn firsthand about the work of the Missionaries of Charity, they are asked to begin by praying in the chapel. Mother Teresa insists that visitors must be greeted with this invitation: "Let us first greet the master of the house. Jesus is here."

Mother Teresa and her community of sisters are not merely activists. They spend much time each day in private prayer and collective worship. Mother Teresa wants to be sure that all members of her community have a strong personal relationship with Jesus. This is crucial, she insists, for their work among the poor:

> I remember one of our sisters who had just come from the university. She came from a well-to-do family.
>
> As we have in our rules, the very next day after the girls have joined the society, they go to the Home for the Dying. Before they went, I told them, "You saw the priest during Mass: with what love, with what delicate care he touched the body of Christ! Make sure you do the same thing when you go to the Home, for Jesus is there in the distressing disguise."
>
> And they went.
>
> After three hours, they came back and one of them, the girl who had come from the university, who had seen so much, so many things, came to my room with such a beautiful smile on her face.
>
> She said, "For three hours I have been touching the body of Christ." And I said, "What did you do, what happened?"
>
> She said, "They brought a man from the street, covered with maggots. And I knew, though I found it very difficult, I knew that I was touching the body of Christ."[2]

This brief story contains a theme that shows up continually in Mother Teresa's conversations: it is important that when we look at the poorest of the poor, we see Jesus in "the distressing disguise." The Gospel text she quotes more than any other is the account of the final judgment in Matthew 25, where the Son of man rewards the righteous because they had fed him when he was hungry, welcomed him when he was a stranger and visited him when he was in prison: "I tell you, just as you did it to one of the least of these who are members of my family, you did it to me" (Mt 25:34-40).

Occupying the Square Inches

Mother Teresa has also influenced my thinking about the relationship of the gospel to social concerns. This has not caused me to give up on Abraham Kuyper. But I do think he needs some help from Mother Teresa.

I have no doubt that Mother Teresa would gladly endorse Kuyper's manifesto: "There is not one square inch of the entire creation about which Jesus Christ does not cry out, 'This is mine! This belongs to me!' " She knows that Jesus has conquered sin. She believes deeply in the ultimate triumph of the cross.

But Mother Teresa does not see the square inches Jesus has redeemed as territory that we must now triumphantly claim as our prize. She knows that many of those square inches are presently occupied by people with stinking, rotting flesh, by grieving parents, by frightened children—the abused, the abandoned, the persecuted and the desperately poor. And she is convinced that our "claiming" those places in the name of Christ means that we must go out to join him "in the distressing disguise" as he makes the agony of the suffering ones his very own.

The square inches for which Christ died are still often very lonely and desolate places. And we must be willing to take our place in those situations, knowing that "in all these things we are more than conquerors through him who loved us."

Some people have criticized Mother Teresa for her highly individualized response to poverty. They think she concentrates too much on one-to-one relationships and not enough on oppressive *systems*. There may be something to that criticism; we do need to be on guard against a tendency in that direction. But I have found her to be a helpful corrective to a very different sort of error.

Mother Teresa has helped me understand why the triumphalist spirit has no place in the life of convicted civility. Treating other people with the gentleness and reverence of Jesus requires that we be deeply sensitive to the pain and brokenness of a creation that has not yet been fully delivered from its cursedness.

Kuyper loved to focus on the victorious King who ascended in power to his heavenly throne. Mother Teresa asks us to look for the Savior who still suffers among the poor and oppressed. Both are asking us, in different ways, to commit ourselves to the service of the triumphant Lord. We need to listen to both of them if we are to nurture a convicted civility. And they need to listen to each other. Abraham Kuyper, meet Mother Teresa!

13
Serving a
Slow God

Civility and the End of Time

• • •

MICK THE WELDER worried a lot about my soul, and he had a very gruff way of showing his concern. Indeed, as I reflect now, many years later, upon the conversations we had, I realize that Mick was rather uncivil in some of the things he said to me. But thinking about what he said helps me to see how our view of God shapes our attitudes toward civility.

Mick had a welding shop down the road from a little restaurant where I worked part-time during my student days. Every day he came in for lunch, and he liked to talk to me about spiritual things. He knew I was studying at the local Reformed seminary, and that made him very suspicious of my theology.

Mick had grown up in the Dutch Reformed church, but he claimed that he never heard the gospel preached there. One day he had had a profound spiritual experience through the ministry of a fundamentalist church. He felt that his life had been changed instantaneously—and he wanted everyone to have that experience.

So Mick would quiz me on my spiritual state. It became a kind of daily ritual:

"Are you saved, fella?"

"Yes, I am, Mick."

"How do you *know* that you're saved?"

Here I would try to throw him off by showing that I could quote the Scriptures. Romans 10:9 was a favorite: "If you confess with your lips that Jesus is Lord and believe in your heart that God raised him from the dead, you will be saved."

"Don't try to be smart with me, fella. You know that isn't good enough. You've got to tell me the day and the hour."

"Mick, I don't *know* the day and the hour when I first became a Christian."

Now his face would show some pain: "You could be in big trouble with the Lord, fella. I hope you know that!"

On the surface it seems that my arguments with Mick were about our differing views of conversion. But they were really arguments about how God works. Mick had a very *fast* God. His God acted in very abrupt, decisive ways. When that God does something, you are not likely to be confused about when it happened!

Mick's God wasn't very patient. And when we think we serve a fast, impatient God, we're not likely to waste much time being civil.

The Divine Pace

As a teenager I read J. B. Phillips's spiritual classic *Your God Is Too Small.* I can't remember any of the book's content, but Phillips's title has served well as a reference point for my thinking about who God is. Throughout my adult life I have regularly asked myself what variation on Phillips's title best summarizes my most recent spiritual experiences. If I had to write a book about the latest developments in my theology, using the "Your God Is Too _____" formula, how would I fill in the blank?

In the 1960s I came to see that my understanding of God had been too "white" and too "American." During the next decade I thought much about how I and my closest spiritual kin have often seen God in very "Western" terms, ignoring the cross-cultural implications of the gospel. The 1980s were a time to think about whether our doctrine of God has been distorted by an overreliance on the categories of maleness. God is the divine Father, to be sure; but God also births us, nurtures us and protects us as a mother watches over her little ones.

Obviously, none of these theological lessons is something I mastered once and for all. They are all matters for ongoing reflection. But if I had to choose a variation on Phillips's title to capture my most recent exercises in corrective spirituality, it would be this: "Your God Is Too Fast."

Mick the welder was mainly interested in the way his fast God dealt with individuals. But the question of God's "pace" has broader implications too. This was brought home to me in a striking fashion at the lunch table during an ecumenical consultation a few years ago. The small group at my table happened to be made up of evangelicals and Roman Catholics. Somehow the question of "creation science" came up.

While none of the evangelicals present was a defender of a

literal six-day creation, we all had close ties to people who are fond of literalist interpretations. So we tried to put the best face we could on the literal-creationist perspective for our Catholic friends.

The Catholics were hard put to generate any sympathy at all for the position we were outlining. Finally, one Catholic scholar threw her hands up in despair, exclaiming in an agitated voice, "Don't these people realize that God likes to do things *slowly*?" Her question brought the issues into sharp focus for me. She meant it as a rhetorical question, but she was actually raising an important point about evangelical spirituality. We evangelicals do *not* take it for granted that God does things slowly. In fact, we think that God likes to work fast. The only proper way of honoring God as the Creator of all things is to assume that everything was created quickly.

My guess is that my theologian friend would have had the same response to Mick the welder's theology of individual conversion: Doesn't he realize that God likes to do things *slowly*?

I never talked to Mick about how he thought the world was created. But I would be surprised if he was anything but a quick-creationist. I imagine that his understanding of God's "macro" activity would be in sync with his views about God's "micro" activity.

The Patient God

I am not completely opposed to the idea of a fast God. I believe in instantaneous conversion—I have seen it happen. I also believe that sometimes God answers our prayers very quickly and decisively. God sometimes heals people's illnesses in dramatic fashion. Relationships can display surprising infusions of God's reconciling power.

That God *sometimes* works fast is a "given" in my theology. But I have trouble with the idea that God's *normal* pace is fast. It's dangerous to insist that God always, or usually, operates in a quick and decisive manner.

The fast-God theology distorts our understanding, for example, of the patterns of social change. I am convinced that one reason many of my spiritual kinfolk are so reluctant to take questions of racial and economic justice seriously is that the problems in those areas seem so intractable. If God works quickly and decisively, then the fact that these problems haven't been solved yet must mean that God doesn't care very much about these particular areas of human concern.

I believe God does care deeply about such issues. The fact that God doesn't offer "quick-fix" solutions to the injustice and oppression that plague the creation is no reason to posit an attitude of divine indifference.

The Mennonites have a nice phrase that is helpful here. They say that we are living "in the time of God's patience." For God's own good reasons he has not yet ushered in the eternal kingdom. God is presently showing patience toward the human race, providing the unsaved with the opportunity to repent and the saved with the opportunity to learn the ways of obedience.

My Roman Catholic friends also have a helpful saying. It comes from St. Ignatius: "God uses crooked sticks to draw straight lines." Even though we haven't yet been perfected, God uses us to work his purposes. We do not need to see the details of the Big Picture. It's enough that we yield ourselves to be instruments of God's mysterious purposes.

"It is his work," Mother Teresa told a *Time* interviewer a few years ago. "I am like a little pencil in his hand. He does the thinking. He does the writing. The pencil has nothing to do with it. The pencil has only to be allowed to be used."[1]

Serving a Slow God

These slower-God perspectives share a strong sense of the importance of God's *providence*. In his wisdom, God has decided to take historical development seriously. Human history is a crucial arena for the working out of God's purposes. And it is necessary that we attune ourselves to this divine pattern.

A healthy sense of God's slow providence is necessary for the life of convicted civility. We must share in the divine patience.

How do we manifest public patience? Here are some traits we need for living as public selves in the time of God's patience.

Flexibility. Joshua Verin's perversity made Roger Williams see the need to be more flexible in making use of his favorite categories. Williams had founded Rhode Island with the hope of making it a bastion of religious liberty. "Freedom of conscience" was his watchword. But even Williams had a hard time tolerating Joshua Verin's strange conscience.

Verin had come to Rhode Island in 1637 from Salem, Massachusetts, and he moved right next door to Roger Williams. Initially Verin had been given a warm welcome by his new neighbors in Rhode Island. When he complained about the oppressively rigid communal standards he had experienced in Massachusetts, they knew exactly what he was talking about. They had come to Rhode Island because of similar experiences.

After a while, though, it became clear to Williams and the other neighbors that Verin was a very unpleasant man who cruelly abused his wife, Ann, on a regular basis. When they confronted their neighbor on this matter, Verin insisted that Ann was only receiving what she deserved, since she spent too much time at church functions.

Williams and his friends were not impressed with Verin's defense. They tried to convince him that he was infringing on his wife's conscience by attempting to restrict her behavior. But Verin was not moved by their arguments. It is God's will, he responded, that wives must submit to their husbands—an imperative that his wife needed help in obeying. He wasn't restricting Ann's religious liberty at all; instead, he was simply helping his wife to live in closer conformity to the divine pattern. His neighbors should stop meddling and allow him to live by his own lights.

The Verin case was finally brought to a vote at the town meeting, and the assembly ruled against Joshua Verin. Soon Verin moved his family back to Salem, Massachusetts. He had decided that, compared to Rhode Island, Massachusetts actually had considerable religious liberty after all.[2]

I admire the Rhode Islanders greatly for their dedication to religious toleration. But their confrontation with Joshua Verin demonstrates that it isn't always easy to promote that cause, even when you are firmly dedicated to it. Verin was not only a wicked man—he was in all likelihood *sincerely* wicked. He undoubtedly believed that God was quite happy with his management of the Verin household. Ann Verin, however, had a rather different view of the situation. To allow Joshua to practice his religion freely was to place unfair—and indeed very cruel—restrictions on her freedom of religion.

I appreciate Williams's willingness to adjust his perspective in the light of this case. He started out with a strict dichotomy between public behavior and private religious conviction. As a champion of religious liberty, he didn't want governments to meddle with matters that are properly decided by the individual conscience. And he was inclined to subsume all religious beliefs under the category of "the private."

But the Verin case made Williams see that he needed to be flexible in applying "public" and "private" categories. The way Joshua treated Ann was not—despite Joshua's arguments—a purely "private" affair. Here was a situation where religious conviction had public implications.

My guess is that flexibility did not come easily to Williams in this situation. He had been through long battles with the Massachusetts Puritans on the subject of liberty, and it must have pained him to take a strong stand against someone who claimed to be acting on private religious convictions. But Williams was more concerned about Ann Verin's pain than about Joshua Verin's conscience, and he was willing to adjust his principles to fit this situation.

Ad hoc adjustments are necessary for all of us. We are on a pilgrimage, and our favorite formulas are often nothing more than helpful summaries of what we have seen thus far. We have to be open to new challenges as we continue in our journey.

Tentativeness. John Stott likes to urge Christians to be "conservative radicals." We have to be conservative about only one thing—our commitment to the gospel. We need to "conserve" the truth of God's Word at all cost. And from that vantage point, Stott says, we need to subject everything else to "radical" critique.

That is a helpful reminder. Our fundamental allegiance is to the gospel alone. In the light of that basic allegiance, all other commitments must be tentative.

Obviously this isn't a call to be cynical in our attitude toward truth or unreliable in our relationships with others. A commitment to forthrightness and fidelity is itself a part of what the gospel requires of us.

One thing it does mean, however, is that we must not be drawn into strong *ideological* attachments. Convicted people are easily captivated by polarized positions, but Christian disciples ought to be very suspicious of hard-line identifications with either "left" or "right."

Take the debate over how to combat poverty. Many liberals favor government intervention on behalf of the poor and the marginalized—welfare programs, affirmative-action policies and the like. Many conservatives argue, on the other hand, that these efforts often do not end up helping the poor. Not every program that is *intended* to benefit the poor actually *does* so; indeed, interventionist solutions often make matters worse in the long run. Furthermore, some policies and systems do not specifically aim at bettering the lot of the oppressed but may in the end produce beneficial effects for them; poverty-stricken people are often served better by the production of wealth than they are by redistributionist programs.

I have much sympathy for the conservative argument on this point. I too am skeptical about many interventionist programs. But we must be careful not to become too rigid. It is also true that sometimes interventionist solutions do deliver on what they promise. Furthermore, not all wealth production does in fact benefit the poor in the long run.

All of this means that we must develop a spirit of caution about programmatic "solutions" offered in the name of the gospel. Does this leave us with no reference points for evaluating proposed programs? Not at all. The God of the Bible does want us to commit ourselves to the cause of the poor and the oppressed. And a serious, long-term focus on the needs of the poor is itself an important reference point in formulating public policy.

Certainly we must continue to discuss who among the wretched of the earth are most in need of our direct ministry of compassion and empowerment. And this discussion should be fueled by a sense of commitment and urgency—a willingness to take informed risks.

Christians can play a very important role in seeing to it that these dialogs take place. And we will be most effective if we ourselves are tentative in our attitudes toward various ideological camps.

Humility. The recognition that God's standards of truth and morality are the only reliable reference points for our lives should instill in us a humble spirit. Arrogant self-righteousness must have no place in our hearts. It's one thing to believe that God's revelation is the only sure and certain guide for our journey; it's another thing to act as if we ourselves possessed a sure and certain grasp of all the complexities of revealed truth.

The ultimate triumph of sanctifying grace in our lives will occur only when we have cast off the triumphalist spirit. The triumph we await is not our triumph, but the victory of the Lamb before whom we will all bow and join in the chorus of voices declaring that Jesus alone is Lord.

Humility is the only fitting attitude for creatures who are on their way to the fullness of God's kingdom. To be sure, there is also room for prophetic critique in our struggles with the crucial issues of modern life. But those corrective words must be spoken humbly, for we ourselves have fled to the cross for healing and correction—and, having experienced there some measure of repair, are emboldened to point others to the Source of the tender mercies that have touched our lives.

Humility also means a refusal to do the final judging about who is "in" and who is "out." God will someday separate the tares from the wheat. Until that day comes, we must approach every encounter with our fellow human beings with the awareness that the Lord is "slow to anger and abounding in steadfast love and faithfulness" (Ps 86:15).

Awe. In their much discussed book *Habits of the Heart,* Robert Bellah and his coauthors explore the possibilities of cultivating civility—they call it "civic friendship"—in our highly individualistic culture. At one point they suggest that perhaps "the most important thing of all" in our attempts to cultivate civility is "common worship, in which we express our gratitude and wonder in the face of the mystery of being itself."[3]

The connection between the mystery of worship and the practice of civility may not be immediately obvious—but it is there. To worship the God of the Scriptures is to bow in the presence of unsurpassed mystery. It is not surprising that the apostle Paul, as he concludes his difficult discussion about the relationship between Jews and Christians, suddenly breaks forth into a hymn to God's mysterious purposes:

O the depth of the riches and wisdom and knowledge of God! How unsearchable are his judgments and how inscrutable his ways!

"For who has known the mind of the Lord?

Or who has been his counselor?" (Rom 11:33-34)

It is important, of course, not merely to acknowledge the fact of divine mystery—we must also take comfort in the assurance that the God of all mystery has invited us to *worship* him, to eat and drink with him and to hear his words of life. In our worship we come into intimate contact with the divine patience. We are not left to guess at his mysterious purposes from a great distance. His love reaches out and draws us to his sheltering arms, where we learn firsthand of his mercy and grace—and where we also learn how to be, in the time of the divine patience, gentle and reverent agents of the gospel in the larger world.

Modesty. Sharing in God's patience means being modest in what we expect of other people. The need for modesty was once impressed upon me in a dramatic way by the sociologist Peter Berger. At a meeting we were both attending, I made a statement—this was in my younger days!—that every Christian is called to engage in radical obedience to God's program of justice, righteousness and peace.

Berger observed that I was operating with a rather grandiose notion of "radical obedience." Somewhere in a retirement home, he said, there is a Christian woman whose greatest fear in life is that she will be humiliated by being unable to control her bladder in the cafeteria line. For this woman, the greatest act of radical obedience to Jesus Christ is to place herself in the hands of a loving God every time she goes off for a meal.

Berger's point was profound. God calls us to deal with the challenges before us, and often our most "radical" challenges are very "little" ones. Many times the call to radical obedience may mean patiently listening to someone who is boring or irritating, treating a fellow sinner with a charity that it is not easy to muster or offering detailed advice on a matter that seems trivial to everyone but the person who requested the advice.

Encounters of this sort can be important occasions for reminding ourselves that we're not asked to duplicate the epic work of the Lamb of God who takes away the sins of the world. The world already has one very adequate Savior. We are called to find our modest places in his larger program and to celebrate the signs of his gracious work wherever we see them— even, and perhaps especially, when their appearance is the occasion for puzzlement and wonder. This is what civility comes to, finally: *an openness to God's surprises.* When that openness marks our lives, we have learned patience—along with the flexibility and tentativeness and humility and awe and modesty that will inevitably come to the patient heart. And since none of this is possible without a clear sense of who we are, and to whom we belong, the patient heart will also be a place where convictedness has found its home.

Notes

Chapter 1: Convicted Civility

[1]*The Poems of W. B. Yeats,* ed. Richard J. Finneran (New York: Macmillan, 1983), 187.

[2]J. Anthony Lukas, "Something's Gone Terribly Wrong in New York," a review of *The Closest of Strangers: Liberalism and the Politics of Race in New York,* by Jim Sleeper. *New York Times Book Review,* Sept. 9, 1990, p. 11.

[3]Martin E. Marty, *By Way of Response* (Nashville: Abingdon Press, 1981), 81.

[4]Corrie ten Boom, with John and Elizabeth Sherrill, *The Hiding Place* (Washington Depot, Conn.: Chosen Books, 1971), 94-95.

[5]John Calvin, *The Institutes of the Christian Religion,* trans. John Allen, 2 vols. (Philadelphia: Westminster Press, n.d.), IV, xx, 2.

Chapter 4: Speaking in God's Presence

[1]Abraham Yeselson and Anthony Gaglione, "What Really Happened When Arafat Spoke at the U.N.," *Worldview* 18 (Mar. 1975), 55.

[2]*Early Quaker Writings,* ed. Hugh Barbour and Arthur Roberts (Grand Rapids, Mich.: Eerdmans, 1973), 269-89.

[3]John H. Yoder, *When War Is Unjust: Being Honest in Just-War Thinking* (Minneapolis: Augsburg, 1984), 20-22.

[4]Gustavo Gutierrez, *A Theology of Liberation: History, Politics and Salvation,* trans. Caridad Inda and John Eagleson (Maryknoll, N.Y.: Orbis, 1973), 206.

Chapter 5: Open Hearts

[1]*Documents of Vatican II*, ed. Austin P. Flannery (Grand Rapids, Mich.: Eerdmans, 1975), 903.

Chapter 6: What's Good About Pluralism?

[1]On Diederichs's thought, see Dunbar Moodie, *The Rise of Afrikanerdom: Power, Apartheid and the Afrikaner Civil Religion* (Berkeley: University of California Press, 1975), 156-59.

[2]For a more detailed discussion of various forms of pluralism, see the study that I have coauthored with Sander Griffioen, *Pluralisms and Horizons: An Essay in Christian Public Philosophy* (Grand Rapids, Mich.: Eerdmans, 1992).

Chapter 8: The Challenge of Other Religions

[1]Simone Weil, *Waiting for God*, trans. Emma Craufurd (San Francisco: Harper and Row, 1973), 69.

[2]S. Mark Heim, *Is Christ the Only Way? Christian Faith in a Pluralistic World* (Valley Forge, Pa.: Judson, 1985), 150.

[3]Stephen Neill, *Christian Faith and Other Faiths* (Downers Grove, Ill.: Inter-Varsity Press, 1984), 124.

Chapter 9: Christian Leadership in a Pluralistic World

[1]James MacGregor Burns, *Leadership* (New York: Harper and Row, 1978), 446.

[2]Burns, *Leadership*, 20.

[3]George F. Will, *Statecraft as Soulcraft: What Government Does* (New York: Simon and Schuster, 1983), 65, 81.

[4]Burns, *Leadership*, 20.

[5]Max DePree, *Leadership Is an Art* (New York: Doubleday, 1989), 9.

Chapter 10: When There Is No "On the Other Hand"

[1]National Conference of Catholic Bishops, *The Challenge of Peace: God's Promise and Our Response—A Pastoral Letter on War and Peace* (Washington, D.C.: United States Catholic Conference, 1983), 42-43.

[2]Augustine of Hippo, *Letters*, trans. Sister Wilfred Parsons (New York: Fathers of the Church, 1953), 3:138.

Chapter 11: Is Hell Uncivil?

[1]Peter Toon, *Heaven and Hell: A Biblical and Theological Overview* (New York: Thomas Nelson, 1986).

[2]John R. Sachs, "Current Eschatology: Universal Salvation and the Problem of Hell," *Theological Studies* 52 (June 1991): 234.

[3]G. C. Berkouwer, *The Return of Christ,* trans. James Van Oosterom (Grand Rapids, Mich.: Eerdmans, 1972), 423.

Chapter 12: Abraham Kuyper, Meet Mother Teresa

[1]For studies of Kuyper's thought and career, see McKendree R. Langley, *The Practice of Political Spirituality: Episodes from the Public Career of Abraham Kuyper, 1879-1918* (Jordan Station, Ont., Canada: Paideia, 1984); and L. Praamsma, *Let Christ Be King: Reflections on the Life and Times of Abraham Kuyper* (Jordan Station, Ont., Canada: Paideia, 1985).

[2]Mother Teresa of Calcutta, *My Life for the Poor,* ed. Jose Luis Gonzalez-Balada and Janet N. Playfoot (San Francisco: Harper and Row, 1985), 18.

Chapter 13: Serving a Slow God

[1]"A Pencil in the Hand of God," interview with Mother Teresa, *Time,* December 4, 1989, p. 11.

[2]This story is found in William G. McLoughlin, *Rhode Island: A Bicentennial History* (New York: W. W. Norton, 1978), 10-11.

[3]Robert Bellah et al., *Habits of the Heart: Individualism and Commitment in American Life* (Berkeley: University of California Press, 1985), 295.

DATE DUE